Bank Expansion in Virginia

1962–1966

BANK EXPANSION

IN VIRGINIA, 1962-1966

The Holding Company and

the Direct Merger

Paul L. Foster

THE UNIVERSITY PRESS OF VIRGINIA

CHARLOTTESVILLE

STUDIES IN BUSINESS ADMINISTRATION
The publication of this study has been assisted by the
Tayloe Murphy Institute and the Graduate School of
Business Administration of the University of Virginia.

First published 1971

ISBN: 0-8139-0338-6
Library of Congress Catalog Card Number: 74-163979
Printed in the United States of America

Contents

Tables, Figures, and Factor Sheets

Foreword

DURING the last decade or two the structure of financial institutions in the United States has experienced as rapid and violent an upheaval as it has known during the history of the Republic. Types of business once thought sacrosanct to commercial banks alone, or to mutual funds or to insurance companies or to savings banks or to investment bankers, have almost without exception been invaded from outside by other institutions. Types of institutions once deemed immutably separate have been merged or brought under common control in other ways. Governmental regulations have changed, barriers separating financial from nonfinancial business have eroded, and the make-up of gross income in most types of financial institutions has altered radically, as have the types of services they offer, their internal structure and their sources of capital.

The Bank Holding Company Act of 1956 is a good point from which to date the revolution, since commercial banking has been close to the center of the convulsion. The financial pages of the press almost daily confirm the continuance of the upheaval, and it seems unlikely that any man now living will see the reestablishment of the degree of stability in financial markets and in the structure of financial institutions that prevailed in the first three decades of this century—not that a period can be termed either placid or stagnant that saw the establishment of the Federal Reserve System, the First World War and the Stock Market Crash of 1929.

Bank Expansion in Virginia, 1962–1966 examines one small segment of this revolution—the wave of bank mergers and acquisitions triggered by the passage in 1962 of the Buck-Holland Bill. This act, with some rather minor restrictions, permitted statewide branch banking. In particular, the study focuses on considerations that influenced two bank managements when choosing between alternative methods of expansion—direct merger and the holding company. The two managements weighed virtually the same elements in making their decisions: the law, market position, economies of operation, costs and sources of financing, future prospects. One management chose direct merger, the other the holding company.

This type of problem is not one which general banking theory handles easily or effectively. Nor is the literature on banking structure, which mostly deals with differences between unit banks and banks with branches, particularly helpful in providing an understanding of what in fact happened. Indirectly the monograph illustrates a good many things about commercial bank management— outside as well as inside Virginia—during the last fifty years and, indeed, sheds light on a number of facets of management in other types of financial institutions. In many respects the study is a clear example of how the best executive thinking in an industry can reverse itself completely between one generation and the next, of how management can and does adapt itself to changes thrust upon it from the outside, and how it sometimes benefits from profit opportunities it did not itself create.

The continued expansion of large banking systems in Virginia and the passage of Public Law 91–67 regulating one-bank holding companies have beeen major developments since 1966. Both of these developments make the subject of this study a matter of current significance. A critical comparison of the holding company and direct merger as alternative methods of expansion is particularly meaningful to bankers in Virginia and other states where the legislative environment is favorable to either method. Furthermore, the enactment of Public Law 91–67 has closed the legislative loophole which made the one-bank holding company a popular and unique form of organization for expansion into nonbanking fields. As a result, the issues examined in this study regarding the alternative forms of organization for bank expansion have been brought into clearer perspective in terms of the more narrowly defined character of bank expansion specified under the current legislation.

In a larger context the study illustrates the extent to which the legislative environment shapes the form and organization of commercial banking, the type and extent of competition, and the range of services it provides the public. This relationship necessarily becomes of vital interest to commercial bankers in states where there has recently been a change in the law, or where a change is likely in the near future. Similarly the analysis indicates how and why the particular form of development and expansion undertaken by an individual bank is more apt to be shaped by the circumstances in which it finds itself than by general advantages or disadvantages suggested by economic or organization theory.

Charles C. Abbott, *Dean*
Graduate School of Business
Administration
University of Virginia

February 1971

Preface

THIS study deals with the mechanism of commercial bank expansion. The setting is Virginia between 1962 and 1966, when a revolution in the banking structure of the state took place. The focus is on two prominent banking organizations: First and Merchants National Bank and United Virginia Bankshares Incorporated, both of Richmond.

With enactment in 1962 of legislation liberalizing branch banking, bank management in Virginia could choose direct merger, the holding company, or a combination of the two as a method of expansion. For this reason, Virginia provides a unique opportunity to study the factors involved in these different methods. The managements of the two banks studied were presumed to have been influenced by similar legislative and economic conditions and to have considered basically the same factors in deciding on a form of organization for expansion. Nevertheless, they made different decisions. Inasmuch as each sought to achieve the general goal of statewide expansion, this research is concerned with the central issues considered by the managements in their decisions to expand by direct merger or the holding company and with the way in which these issues were assessed.

In exploring these questions the literature is reviewed, and the direct merger experiences of First and Merchants National Bank and the holding company experiences of United Virginia Bankshares are evaluated as guides for management action. Where a disparity is apparent between the literature and management action, an attempt is made to determine whether this difference provides a basis for improved insights into the issues. By this method, the structure of the analysis appraises the relative merits of the two methods of expansion. However, the analysis is not intended to judge management's actions in a normative sense.

An underlying premise is that some of the advantages and disadvantages of the two forms as advanced in the literature actually do not apply in practice and that the individual circumstances of each organization may account for this discrepancy. If this premise is correct, the examination of the central issues considered by management should provide useful information to other banks anticipating expansion. The findings may also be relevant to legislators in other states where statute changes permitting unit or limited branching could result in expansion by both direct merger and holding company. In 1966 there were thirty-three states where such changes were possible including Ohio, Texas, Illinois, and Wisconsin.[1]

There were several reasons for the decision to study First and Merchants National Bank, a merged system, and United Virginia Bankshares, a holding company, from among the six major Virginia banking organizations involved in statewide expansion during the period 1962–66.[2] Among the four Virginia holding companies that could have been studied, United Virginia Bankshares (hereafter referred to as Bankshares) had the clearest option to select either method of expansion. Bankshares had not filed with the Securities and Exchange Commission to form its holding company prior to the introduction in January 1962 of state legislation that authorized expansion by direct merger.[3] By way of contrast, First Virginia and Financial General, both holding companies, were operating in Virginia before the 1962 legislation. Consequently, they were already committed to a particular method of expansion. The remaining organization, Virginia Commonwealth, had already decided to form a holding company when the General Assembly opened on January 10, 1962.[4] Liberalized legislation to permit branching was introduced into the General Assembly on January 18, 1962, and became effective July 1, 1962.

First and Merchants National Bank (hereafter referred to as First and Merchants), like Bankshares, had the opportunity to select either method of expansion. It had not made a final decision on a method of expansion prior to the enactment of the 1962 legislation.[5] Both Bankshares and First and Merchants made their de-

[1] In 1966 the thirty-three states with statutes on unit and limited branching accounted for 88 percent of the 13,785 banks and 79 percent of the $410 billion of total deposits in the United States.

[2] The major systems involved in statewide expansion during the period 1962–66 were: by merger, First and Merchants National Bank of Richmond and Virginia National Bank of Norfolk; by holding company, Financial General Corporation of Washington, D.C., First Virginia Bankshares Corporation of Arlington, United Virginia Bankshares Incorporated of Richmond, and Virginia Commonwealth Bankshares Corporation of Richmond. The First National Exchange Bank of Roanoke is not included because it served only the southwestern region of the state. With Metropolitan National Bank of Richmond it formed a new holding company in 1967—Dominion Bankshares Corporation.

[3] Lewis B. Flinn, Jr., personal communication, 1968.

[4] Thomas C. Boushall, personal communication, 1968.

[5] John Green, personal communication, 1968.

cisions to expand during approximately the same period. Consequently, their decisions were made under similar external environmental conditions. Furthermore, the organizations were alike with regard to location, size, and expansion strategy. Both were large Richmond organizations with extensive correspondent systems and both had worked actively for the liberalization of legislation for bank branching in 1962.

By way of contrast, Virginia National Bank of Norfolk, the second major merged system, did not offer so clear a comparison with Bankshares as did First and Merchants. Its location and expansion strategy were different from those of Bankshares in that Virginia National, with the home office in Norfolk, had expanded into both rural and metropolitan areas of the state, whereas Bankshares, with the home office in Richmond, had concentrated on the metropolitan areas.[6]

The field research for this study was conducted from the management point of view. It focused on the problem of selecting either direct merger or the holding company as a method of expansion. It involved executives responsible for planning and carrying out the expansion decisions while they were still active in their organizations and while expansion was still in progress. The timing of the study made possible the examination of the important issues while they were still current.

There are good reasons for regarding the period 1962–66 as sufficiently long to reflect many of the underlying trends in the Virginia banking structure. The wave of mergers and holding company acquisitions is not likely to continue for an extended time since the number of banks eligible for acquisition is being reduced. Moreover, as the merger and holding company movement matures, banks expanding on a statewide basis are likely to approach the geographic limits of their expansion plans.

This research has several major limitations. First, it does not encompass all of the major statewide banking systems in Virginia. Second, the focus of the field research is limited to a single point of view—that of management. Consequently, the scope of the field research does not investigate management considerations or actions in the context of standards of public welfare, or public benefit, except insofar as management considered them. However, this limitation does not apply to the analysis of management's expansion experiences. Here the points of view of other interested parties—such as stockholders and customers—are considered. Third, the findings and conclusions may require modification with more

[6] R. Cosby Moore, personal communication, 1968.

experience. The advantages and disadvantages of one form of banking organization may change as the result of future state or national legislation or after the merger and holding company activity in Virginia slows down. A fourth limitation concerns the use of quantitative data primarily for descriptive purposes. The study does not include in-depth analysis supporting or contradicting previous research in areas such as economies of scale, performance-to-structure relationships, and concentration-to-competition relationships.

I wish to acknowledge the interest and support of the banking community in the conduct of my research. I am most indebted to Professor Charles Abbott, dean of the Graduate School of Business Administration at the University of Virginia, for his guidance and patience during the preparation of the dissertation from which this book is adapted. Thomas C. Boushall, director emeritus and honorary chairman of the board of the Bank of Virginia, contributed much to the material on the history of banking in Virginia. Others who gave both time and invaluable information were A. Halsey Cook, executive vice president, First National City Bank of New York; Frederick Deane, Jr., president, the Bank of Virginia; Lewis B. Flinn, Jr., vice president-treasurer, United Virginia Bankshares Incorporated; John Green, vice president, First and Merchants National Bank; Aubrey Heflin, first vice president, Federal Reserve Bank of Richmond; E. T. Holland, chairman of the board, First Virginia Corporation; Coleman C. McGehee, Executive vice president, First and Merchants National Bank; and R. Cosby Moore, chairman of the board, Virginia National Bank. Charles O. Meiburg and the staff of the Bureau of Population and Economic Research at the University of Virginia provided essential statistical data and administrative support.

I acknowledge with gratitude permission to reprint material from Lewis B. Flinn, Jr., vice president-treasurer, United Virginia Bankshares Incorporated, and also from *American Banker,* the Board of Governors of the Federal Reserve System, Columbia University Press, the Charlottesville (Va.) *Daily Progress, Commonwealth,* the Federal Reserve Bank of Richmond, *Law and Contemporary Problems,* the Michie Company, the National Industrial Conference Board, the Richmond *Times-Dispatch,* Rutgers University Press, the *Wall Street Journal,* and the *Washington and Lee Law Review.*

PAUL L. FOSTER

Charlottesville, Virginia
July 1971

Bank Expansion in Virginia

1962–1966

I *Introduction*

T HE controversy underlying changes in state legislation regulating bank expansion involves the *unit* versus *branch* issue.

Probably there is no older or deeper banking controversy than that between the proponents of unit banking, who believe such a system is essential to the maintenance of competition and the preservation of small banks, and the proponents of branch banks, who insist that efficiency and stability require multi-office institutions.[1]

The purpose here, however, is not to judge the relative merits of unit versus branch banking per se or the diversity of state legislation, which reflects the many attitudes toward this issue. Rather it is to develop a historical perspective of the environmental factors and forces that influenced Virginia bankers in their deliberations over an apporpriate banking structure for the state.

THE 1922–1962 PERIOD

1922–1928. The events of 1922–28 culminated in the passage of legislation restricting branch banking in 1928. Two features were salient in this period. First, state-chartered banks in Virginia could open new (*de novo*) branches throughout the state, whereas national banks were prohibited from branching under previous interpretations of the National Bank Act of 1864.[2] The second feature centered on the situation of the Morris Plan Bank of Richmond, now the Bank of Virginia. This was the only bank in the state that had established *de novo* branches in large cities other than its home office in Richmond. Furthermore, this bank

---

[1] Commission on Money and Credit, *Private Financial Institutions* (Englewood Cliffs, N.J.: Prentice-Hall, 1963) , p. 47.

[2] Gerald C. Fischer, *American Banking Structure* (New York: Columbia University Press, 1968) . See chapter II for a historical discussion of the development of unit and branch banking, including legislative aspects. National Banks were not permitted to branch under federal law until passage of the McFadden Act in 1927. This law limited branches of national or state member banks to their home cities.

operated under a Morris Plan franchise and not as a regular commercial bank.[3]

The Morris Plan Bank of Richmond was founded in 1922 by Thomas C. Boushall, formerly an officer of the National City Bank of New York.[4] Interested in starting a Morris Plan Bank in Richmond, Boushall received a franchise and financial backing from Arthur J. Morris, who was expanding the plan throughout the country.[5] This bank was unusual in that it had a regular commercial bank charter even though it operated a Morris Plan franchise; it did not, however, take demand deposits or provide other commercial services. Activities were limited to savings accounts and installment loans to individuals and small businesses. Late in 1922 the bank opened a branch in Petersburg. Another branch was opened in Newport News by merger with the Merchants and Mechanics Savings Association in 1925. In 1928 a third branch was opened in Roanoke, and a merger of the Morris Plan Bank of Norfolk made it a branch of the Morris Plan Bank of Richmond.[6]

The branching activities of the Morris Plan Bank of Richmond and its business in consumer installment loans were so inconsistent with the tradition of commercial bankers in Virginia[7] that this bank became anathema to many bankers in the state, whose attitudes were described as being "steeped in tradition."[8] Such attitudes help account for the fact that only one bank in Virginia was branching on an areawide basis during the 1920s. Typical comments of commercial bankers to the chief officer of the Morris Plan Bank of Richmond were that it was poor banking practice and an unnecessary risk to have "someone else lend your money" in branches distant from Richmond; that consumer lending was

[3] A Morris Plan Bank was a financial institution that accepted as deposits only savings accounts and that made only installment loans to individuals. This system of lending was devised by Arthur J. Morris, who is still a director of the Bank of Virginia. In 1910 when Morris opened the original Morris Plan Bank, Fidelity Loan and Trust Company in Norfolk, the availability of credit to average wage earners was almost nonexistent. The original approach to the Morris Plan Bank was designed to fill the need for credit facilities for wage earners throughout the United States, who, generally speaking, were not receiving this service from commercial banks of the day.

[4] Background on the Bank of Virginia was obtained through interviews with Thomas C. Boushall, honorary chairman of the board and founder of the Bank of Virginia, and Frederick Deane, Jr., president of the Bank of Virginia. The bank has had only two chief executive officers since its founding in 1922. Herbert Moseley succeeded Boushall as chief executive in 1959.

[5] Thomas C. Boushall, personal communication, 1968.

[6] *Ibid.*   [7] *Ibid.*   [8] *Ibid.*

neither reliable nor desirable and consequently was a dangerous practice; and that the consumer loan would likely have an unacceptably high default rate.[9]

The lack of enthusiasm for branching was not peculiar to Virginia bankers. In 1922 the American Bankers Association, apparently in response to various proposals to permit branching by national banks, adopted a resolution:

We regard branch banking or the establishment of additional offices by banks as detrimental to the best interest of the people of the United States. Branch banking is contrary to public policy, violates the basic principles of our government and concentrates the credits of the Nation and the power of money in the hands of a few.[10]

Not until 1930 did the American Bankers Association modify its antibranching position.[11]

The geographic and economic character of Virginia provides additional reasons why only one bank in the state engaged in branching in the 1920s. Virginia was divided into distinct regions: Tidewater Virginia—Norfolk, Newport News, Portsmouth—was maritime oriented, Richmond was tobacco oriented, and Northern Virginia was oriented to the federal government. Furthermore, certain areas in the state were closely associated with neighboring states and in some cases still are today: Bristol in the far southwestern corner of the state had close ties with Tennessee, and the isolated Eastern Shore with Maryland. Because the separate areas of Virginia had few economic, political, and social ties with each other, branching across regional boundaries was not attractive to commercial bankers. However, to the Morris Plan Bank of Richmond, branching was an essential strategy. Management in this bank considered it necessary to serve the major population centers, where most of the consumers were located.[12] In contrast, the lack of interest in branching on the part of commercial bankers in Virginia suggests that they were content to maintain the status quo, restricting their business to commercial customers within their individual marketing areas.

As a result of the branching activities of the Morris Plan Bank of Richmond, friction developed with some of the other commercial banks in Virginia. The conflict came into the open early

[9] *Ibid.* On the question of "someone else lending your money," Boushall said that bankers failed to realize a branch was not "someone else" but an extension of the main bank.

[10] Fischer, *American Banking Structure*, p. 45.

[11] *Ibid.*, p. 49.

[12] Boushall, personal communication, 1968,

in 1928 when the Virginia Bankers Association prepared a revision of the existing banking code to submit to the Virginia General Assembly. Provisions of this revision restricted the authority of banks to branch or merge outside of the home area of the parent bank and limited to 4 percent per annum the interest a bank could pay on savings deposits. The Morris Plan Bank of Richmond, a member of the association, was not advised of this proposal while it was being prepared. The revision, inimical to many of the basic policies of this bank, appeared to be specifically aimed at restricting its activities.[13] The Morris Plan Bank of Richmond had paid 5 percent interest since its founding in 1922, a practice regarded by the commercial banks as a threat to their savings deposits, since the rates were generally 3 percent in the Richmond area and 4 percent elsewhere.[14]

The effort to limit branching and savings deposit interest may also have been related to other legislative developments. The action came during the peak of antibranching sentiment at the national level. In the period 1910–30 many states passed legislation prohibiting branches or restricting their location. In 1910 there were eight states with legislation prohibiting branching; by 1930 the number had reached twenty-three, its historic high.[15] Two three-year periods, 1921–23 and 1927–29, account for approximately half of the antibranching legislation enacted by the states between 1910 and 1930.[16] This concentration of antibranching legislation was attributed to the efforts of national banks and of the Comptroller of the Currency to permit branching of national banks. In the 1921–23 period,

Comptroller of the Currency Crissinger requested that Congress pass a limited branch bill for national banks, and when this was not done he began to authorize some of the institutions under his jurisdiction to establish limited service branches in their head-office cities. The impetus these and other actions gave to the antibranch movement in the early 1920's was quite apparent by 1923 in the trial of the St. Louis case. This

---

[13] *Ibid.*

[14] Ibid. The proposal forcibly illustrates the difference in viewpoints between the Morris Plan Bank of Richmond and the commercial bankers in Virginia. It suggests that commercial banks generally were not concerned with the public welfare and that they had no evolving concept of what the commercial banking industry should be; in fact it appears to work against the public welfare since it was aimed at reducing interest paid on savings and restraining the growth of a developing segment of banking intended to provide a source of credit to the consumer.

[15] Fischer, *American Banking Structure,* p. 59.

[16] *Ibid.,* p. 61.

was the first clear test of the branching power of national banks, and the opponents of branching were so effective in convincing their state officials of the importance of this litigation that eleven state attorneys-general filed briefs as *amici curiae,* supporting the position of those opposed to national bank branching.[17]

Between 1927 and 1929 antibranching sentiment again resulted from an effort on the part of national banks to obtain branching privileges equal to those of state banks.

The second interval in which a large number of states prohibited branch banking began with passage of the McFadden Act in 1927 and terminated in 1929. In the 1927 legislation the antibranch forces had won a considerable but not complete victory. Branching by national banks was limited to the head-office city (town, village) and it was allowed only if the relevant state law also permitted state banks to establish and operate branches.[18]

The fact that provisions of the McFadden Act were reflected in the amendment to the statutes proposed by the Virginia Bankers Association supports the assumption that Virginia legislation was influenced by these developments on the national scene. Moreover, the announced plans of the Morris Plan Bank of Richmond to branch into new areas gave specific relevance to the legislation in Virginia.

During the 1928 session of the General Assembly, the chairman of the legislative committee and the secretary of the Virginia Bankers Association called on the president of the Morris Plan Bank of Richmond. At this meeting it was suggested that if the bank's representatives would support the proposed limitation of interest on savings deposits, the legislative committee of the association would undertake to have the code amended specifically to permit branches in cities other than that of the bank's head office, provided the cities had a minimum population of fifty thousand. This compromise was accepted by the Morris Plan Bank and was subsequently incorporated into the 1928 banking code, which established the legislative framework for "limited branching" in Virginia.[19]

---

[17] *Ibid.,* pp. 62–63.   [18] *Ibid.,* pp. 63–64.

[19] Boushall, personal communication, 1968. An ironic twist to this power play by the commercial banks was that the Morris Plan Bank of Richmond wanted to reduce its 5-percent savings rate, yet could not for fear of losing depositors. It so happened that the bank was having a difficult time attracting savings even though 5 percent was paid and most commercial banks paid 3 to 4 percent. A large segment of the saving public shared the feeling that "something must be wrong" if the new bank was paying more than the prestigious

1928 legislation. The legislation approved in 1928 was more re-strictive of branching activities than previous legislation.[20] Spe-cifically, it restricted expansion by *de novo* branches, merger, or purchase to limited geographic areas. The State Corporation Commission was permitted to authorize banks having paid-up and unimpaired capital and surplus of fifty thousand dollars or more:

1. To branch within the limits of the city, town, or village in which the parent bank was located and in any city having a population of not less than fifty thousand inhabitants; and

2. To merge with or purchase a bank within the same or adjoin-ing counties or banks within a distance of twenty-five miles of a parent bank, provided that the banks involved had been in actual operation for a period of two years or more, except that the State Corporation Commission under certain condi-tions could waive this time requirement.[21]

Newport News, Norfolk, Petersburg, Portsmouth, Richmond, and Roanoke met the population criteria for *de novo* branches in the period 1929–48.

1929–1948. During the early years of the 1929–48 period and on through World War II, the volume of commercial bank loans decreased sharply. In the decade of the 1920s total commercial loans of all national banks decreased from just over $10 billion to approximately $7.5 billion.[22] This drop was attributed to a general rollback in commercial borrowing from banks:

Business, influenced among other factors by the cheapness and abundance of long term funds, turned more and more in this period to the securities markets for its capital requirements, and relied less and less upon the banking structure, so that commercial loans declined as bond—and stock —prices increased.[23]

By the end of the 1930s the total of commercial loans of all national banks had fallen to just over $4 billion, a decrease of

---

commercial banks. The Morris Plan Bank of Richmond was looking for a way to solve the "5-percent rate problem" and, at the same time, continue to expand in the more populated areas of the state; therefore, the compromise of rate reduction for limited branching was readily accepted.

[20] As noted earlier, bankers throughout the country in the 1920s and 1930s, were able to affect the course of legislation and thus influence the course of competition in their states.

[21] See Appendix B, Branching Provisions of the 1928 Legislation.

[22] Albert R. Koch, *The Financing of Large Corporations, 1920–1939* (New York: National Bureau of Economic Research, 1943) , p. 69.

[23] Charles Cortez Abbott, *The New York Bond Market, 1920–1939* (Cambridge, Mass.: Harvard University Press, 1937) , p. 153.

approximately $6 billion since 1920.[24] The depression accounted in the 1930s for this continuing downward trend, which persisted through World War II, for corporation assets were highly liquid from war contract profits. The nonessential segments of the business sector found it difficult to replace depleted inventories, and capital outlays were generally for new plant capacity in defense industries. Consequently, commercial bank loans were further liquidated, and banks invested heavily in the government securities market, where the government was using deficit financing for the war effort.

Although during the period 1920–45 commercial bankers had every reason to look for new outlets for loans, most were slow to recognize and respond to the opportunities in consumer finance. As a consequence, the large-scale entry of banks into the field of consumer lending is a comparatively recent development.

Prior to the 1900s such lending was conducted on a highly selective basis. Most banks occasionally extended loans to consumers, but the practice was generally confined to the accommodation of established bank customers, for it was regarded as an exception to established lending policy. The shift in attitude came slowly and erratically among individual banks, but by the end of the 1920s a large number of banks throughout the nation had established personal loan departments.

The National City Bank of New York was the first major commercial bank in the United States to establish a separate department for making small loans, when it inaugurated its Personal Loan Department on May 4, 1928. The general pattern of its initial program was modeled on the Morris Plan, which was inaugurated by Arthur J. Morris as early as 1910 in Norfolk, Virginia. Our bank, however, developed its own forms and internal procedures. Its general objective was to provide loans in modest amounts at reasonable rates, repayable in monthly installments to wage earners, small merchants and others who, at that time, had little or no credit standing in commercial banks. The extension of such credit facilities was a logical outlet for deposits resulting from savings accounts, another service which commercial banks adopted in the twenties.[25]

In the 1930s bank interest in consumer lending was stimulated by the growth of demand for consumer credit associated with the mass appeal of the automobile, the banks' favorable experience in consumer lending under programs of government loan insurance, and the combination of low interest rates, large excess reserves,

---

24 Koch, p. 69.
25 First National City Bank of New York to the author, September 27, 1968.

and application of amortization principles to consumer goods.[26] Also, the economic impact of the depression altered attitudes toward consumer credit. Commercial banks were not making many loans because of the stagnation of the national economy and the reluctance of commercial customers to borrow. However, the depression did not cause as great a decrease in the demand for consumer credit.[27]

During the years 1929–48 commercial banks in Virginia began slowly to expand into the area of consumer finance, and in turn, the Morris Plan Bank of Virginia invited commercial accounts.[28] Thus, head-to-head competition, the salient feature of this period in addition to branching, later contributed to the enactment of even more restrictive legislation on branching in 1948.

Between 1920 and 1940 commercial bankers considered the Morris Plan Bank of Virginia, operating in the installment loan area, nothing more than "a high-class small loan company." An aggravating factor was that commercial bankers traditionally considered it unethical to advertise for loans, an attitude that persisted into the 1930s. The Morris Plan banks, which engaged in extensive advertising, were characterized as "razzle-dazzle promoters" because they gave away merchandise to obtain accounts. While such practices are acceptable today, the Morris Plan banks engaged in them at a time when they were considered most improper. (There were no other Morris Plan Banks in Virginia after the conversion of the Morris Plan Bank of Portsmouth into the Commercial Exchange Bank around 1940.) These circumstances reinforced the view of commercial bankers in Virginia that the small Morris Plan Bank of Richmond was not really a bank at all, and certainly not of the stature of a commercial bank.[29]

In 1927 the American Bank and Trust Company of Richmond opened a consumer loan department.[30] This innovation was said to have a startling impact on the banking community in the state and elsewhere.[31] Yet the facts indicate a continuing lack of interest in consumer loans by this bank and by other commercial banks in Virginia. American Bank and Trust located its consumer loan department in the basement, probably to separate its "working

---

[26] Commission on Money and Credit, pp. 162–64.

[27] Boushall, personal communication, 1968.

[28] Name changed from the Morris Plan Bank of Richmond to the Morris Plan Bank of Virginia, July 1, 1928.

[29] Boushall, personal communication, 1968.

[30] *Ibid.*

[31] *Ibid.*

man" business from its "carriage trade."[32] When American Bank and Trust did not reopen after the bank holiday in 1933, the "paper" from its consumer loan department, which was offered to the Morris Plan Bank of Virginia, totaled approximately $116,000 —a negligible amount compared to the latter's $7.5 million.[33] The Morris Plan Bank of Virginia in 1937 held more consumer installment loans than all of Virginia's commercial banks and finance companies combined.[34]

This general lack of interest in consumer credit on the part of Virginia's commercial bankers is confirmed by R. Pierce Lumpkin:

The commercial bank of today is indeed the department store of finance —but it has not always been so. Throughout the 19th century and in the early years of the 20th century, Virginia bankers, along with their fraternity brothers in other parts of the nation, were steeped in the banking principle of note and deposit issue based upon short-term, self-liquidating business credit. True, some loans were made to individuals, for home purchase or for other reasons, but the credit rating had to be of the highest quality. In the early 1920's Virginia bankers still considered the active promotion of banking services for the average individual as outside the area of active competitive pursuit. However, a change was already under way which, although more than two decades were to pass before its fruition, was destined to change the patterns of accepted banking practices more drastically than any previous change in banking's history. This emerging change acknowledged the fact that commercial banking had much to offer to the average individual and that the individual, in large numbers, could make a substantial contribution to bank profits.[35]

In the 1930s, in response to the entry of commercial banks into the area of consumer credit the Morris Plan Bank of Virginia broadened the scope of its services.[36] Initially, the bank began to

[32] Interview with A. Halsey Cook, executive vice president, First National City Bank of New York, October 3, 1968. First National City Bank separated its first consumer loan office from its main office for this reason.

[33] Boushall, personal communication, 1968. Another expression of a commercial bank's attitude toward consumer credit was the effort on the part of a New York correspondent bank to drop the Morris Plan Bank of Virginia's $300,000 line of credit unless loans for automobiles and new office construction were stopped. In 1928 the Morris Plan Bank of Virginia was the first bank in the state to buy dealer automobile paper and in 1935 the first to make extensive direct (over-the-counter) collateral auto loans to consumers.

[34] *Ibid.*

[35] R. Pierce Lumpkin, "Virginia Banking Today: The Quiet Revolution," *The Commonwealth,* March 1965, p. 27.

[36] Boushall, personal communication, 1968. Government-insured FHA home improvement loans were a factor that brought Virginia's commercial banks into the consumer area in 1934.

accept checking accounts of individuals only. Later, commercial checking accounts were accepted, and just before World War II the bank entered the commercial loan field in active competition with the other commercial banks. However, the bank's growth and development as a commercial institution did not really start until after World War II.[37] By 1948 the bank—operating under its present name of the Bank of Virginia—had successfully implemented its strategy of expanding into the commercial area in direct competition with commercial banks. It had grown to be the sixth largest bank in Virginia.[38] Still the only bank in the state that had developed a branch system in cities with a population over fifty thousand, it had plans to expand into new areas as soon as they met the population provisions of the laws on branching.[39]

Out-of-state ownership compounded the unfriendly feeling of the other commercial banks in Virginia toward the Bank of Virginia, for since its founding the major stockholder in the bank had been the holding company established to franchise Morris Plan banks throughout the United States. As late as 1953, when the control of the Bank of Virginia was sold, the holding company still owned 57 percent. This fact was used by the opponents of branching to argue the alleged dangers of out-of-state control.[40] Thus, the move of the Bank of Virginia into the area of commercial accounts, the anticipated expansion of the bank in Alexandria, and the request for approval of a third branch in Norfolk rekindled the branching issue among some of the commercial bankers in the state.[41] For the second time in twenty years the Bank of Virginia, as a major proponent for expansion, was about to play a central role in a controversy over legislation to curb branching.

In February 1948 an editorial reported the issues in the following terms:

[37] Ibid. The bank's name was changed from the Morris Plan Bank of Virginia to the Bank of Virginia on January 1, 1946, in order to qualify more specifically for commercial accounts.

[38] See Appendix A, Table A-1. Tables A-2 and A-3 show the twenty largest banks in Virginia at year-end 1961 and 1968.

[39] Boushall, personal communication, 1968. The Bank of Virginia expected that Alexandria would meet the population requirement after the 1950 census.

[40] Frederick Deane, Jr., personal communication, 1968.

[41] *Ibid.* Deane stated that the Bank of Virginia had grown up "relatively unnoticed" by the other commercial bankers because not until after World War II did it become an aggressive competitor in the commercial accounts area, nor had it been considered a legitimate competitor up to that time.

It is regrettable that the question of the advisability of placing stricter limits on branch banking in Virginia has been raised in a way that makes it difficult for the General Assembly to decide the issue strictly on its merits and from the standpoint of the welfare of the people of Virginia rather than on rival banking interests.[42]

The present status of the matter is that of a fight for advantage between The Bank of Virginia and the members of the Virginia Bankers Association. They are alarmed by the growth of the former and by its apparent inclination to extend its operations into new localities, and they want a law to protect them.[43]

The main contenders in the branching controversy were the Virginia Bankers Association, the advocate for a ban on branching, and the Bank of Virginia, whose operations were singled out as typical of the problems inherent in statewide branch banking.[44] While both the pros and cons of branch banking were aired, the great preponderance of the editorials supported the Bank of Virginia.[45] Most of the arguments cited in the press for and against branch banking were oversimplified. Arguments aired in the press on this subject were that:

1. Branch banking creates a dangerous monopoly, which must be guarded against.

2. The number of banks in a community must be limited so that each one will be strong enough to protect the people.

3. Branch banking creates a much greater opportunity for out-of-state control of Virginia financial institutions.[46]

4. The "unit bank" system is "most consonant with the genius of the American people" and protects against chain or branch monopolies.

[42] The "welfare of the people" in the 1920s and 1930s was nowhere well accepted as a useful criterion for judging the impact of banking legislation on the structure of banking. Before the enactment of the Bank Holding Company Act of 1956 and the Bank Merger Act of 1960 federal statutes provided relatively few guidelines regulating expansion of commercial banks. These statutes now include explicit public interest considerations.

[43] Charlottesville *Daily Progress*, February 7, 1948.

[44] Richmond *Times-Dispatch*, February 9, 1948. Fears of banking monopoly were not new. This argument dates from the 1830s; it involves the questions of banks or no banks, and free banking laws or control of bank charters.

[45] According to the records of the Bank of Virginia there were twenty-two editorials for and none against the position of the proponents of branching.

[46] Many references were made to the out-of-state control of the Bank of Virginia. Control was traced through the Morris Plan Corporation, the American General Corporation, and the Equity Corporation of New York to the Oceanic Trading Company, Inc., a Panama corporation.

5. Branch banking encourages unfettered competition and avoids "closed shop for the bankers union."
6. Branch banking improves service to the people.
7. Legislation should not be passed to limit competition but to encourage it.
8. No legislation should ever be passed against an individual or a specific corporation. Legislation should be aimed at principles.[47]

One observer offered the opinion that the outcome of the 1948 controversy was never really in doubt. The contest between the Bank of Virginia and the Virginia Bankers Association was described as a mismatch:

The contest appears as uneven as any possibly could be. Not only is the Virginia Bankers Association a powerful organization in its own right, but many members of the General Assembly are most certain to be sympathetic with the intent of the legislation. Checking the membership of the Senate, it appears that a majority of the senators are bank attorneys, bank directors, or bank officials. In the House of Delegates, about one-quarter of the members are either officers or directors of banks. Not one member of either the Senate or House, however, is known to be an officer, director, or attorney of The Bank of Virginia.[48]

The antibranching bill was passed by both the Virginia Senate and the House of Delegates by wide margins, and *de novo* branching or merger on a statewide basis was prohibited.[49]

1948 legislation. Changes in the Virginia Code enacted in 1948 and remaining in effect until 1962 eliminated *de novo* branching in cities having a population of fifty thousand or more. The net result of this legislation was the elimination of opportunities for banks to expand outside their home areas. The legislation specified that the State Corporation Commission was permitted to authorize banks having paid-up and unimpaired capital and surplus of $50,000 or more:

1. To branch within the limits of the city, town, or village of the parent bank;[50] and
2. To merge with or purchase a bank within the same or

[47] Richmond *Times-Dispatch,* January 13, February 6, 9, and 18, 1948.
[48] *Ibid.,* January 23, 1948.
[49] *Ibid.,* February 17 and 26, 1948. The bill passed the House by a vote of 70 to 22 and the Senate by a vote of 30 to 8.
[50] "Town or village" are considered the same as "county" for definition of location under the Virginia banking code. The significant location distinction is between "city" and "county."

adjoining counties or located within twenty-five miles of a parent bank,[51] provided that the banks shall have been in operation for a period of five years or more, except that the State Corporation Commission under certain conditions may waive this time requirement.[52]

The 1948 legislation contained a "grandfather" clause specifying that the restrictions did not apply to branch banks established prior to June 29, 1948, or to branches already authorized by the commission but not yet opened. The effect was to allow all branches of the Bank of Virginia in the cities of Newport News, Norfolk, Petersburg, Portsmouth, and Roanoke to continue in operation. The bill also required that bank expansion meet certain conditions not included in previous legislation. Specifically, the State Corporation Commission was permitted to authorize *de novo* branches and mergers "when satisfied that public convenience and necessity will thereby be served."[53] Thus, for the first time, the state law contained an explicit public service requirement for expansion.

1949–1962. In the fourteen years following the 1948 legislation there were efforts to liberalize the requirements for branching. In July 1961 the Richmond *Times-Dispatch* carried the headline: "Curbs on Bank of Virginia Boomerang—Competitors Feel the Pinch of the 1948 Laws." Six months later it carried another headline reading: "Virginia Banks Hamstrung—Laws Curb Expansion."[54] As implied by these headlines, Virginia bankers were finding it increasingly difficult to control their own destiny. A number of developments—specifically, industrial and urban growth throughout the state, competition from large out-of-state banks to the north and south, and concern over the expansion of bank holding companies in the state—were causing some bankers to reappraise the branching issue.

During the years 1948–62 the state was making a rapid transition from a rural to an industrial and urban economy. In 1950 more than half of the population of Virginia lived outside metropolitan areas; by 1960 more than 56 percent lived in urban centers. During this period population in the metropolitan areas increased seven times faster than in the rest of the state, and wages and salaries far outstripped farm income. This rapid growth of Virginia's urban

[51] Under federal and Virginia codes there is no real distinction between merger, purchase, and consolidation of assets.
[52] See Appendix B, Branching Provisions of the 1948 Legislation.
[53] *Ibid.*
[54] Richmond *Times-Dispatch,* July 2, 1961, January 14, 1962.

and industrial communities increased pressure on the state's banks, whose growth was restricted by the 1948 legislation.

In the early 1960s banks in North Carolina, Maryland, and the District of Columbia were larger than banks in Virginia. The greater lending power of these banks was alleged to account for the increasing frequency with which large commercial and industrial projects in Virginia were financed by out-of-state banking institutions. An outstanding example was the financing by a North Carolina bank of the H. K. Porter Company's $2.65 million electrical transformer plant in Lynchburg and its $1.5 to $2 million Disston Saw Division in Danville.[55]

To compete for these larger lines of credit, Virginia's bankers saw the need for larger banking units. In support of this position, the presidents of three large Richmond banks were quoted as saying:

Large industries need large credit lines. The biggest bank in Virginia can offer only $1,550,000. Or consider this: Richmond has four of the six largest banks in the state. Yet all four combined can offer an industry no more than $4,950,000. By contrast, in any of 15 North Carolina cities an industry can obtain five million dollars from a single bank.[56]

Virginia bankers were also faced with increasing competition from a new source—bank holding companies. Expansion of these institutions was not regulated by the Virginia banking code. They were expanding operations, primarily in Northern Virginia, by acquiring banks as affiliates.[57] The acquired banks did not become branches but remained separate units of the holding company under federal laws and under the supervision of the Federal Reserve System. Consequently, holding companies had a competitive advantage over banks with regard to expansion:

The two biggest banks in Winchester will be acquired by holding companies, if present negotiations are successful, and Virginia bankers will have another reason to ponder their course for the future. . . .

Group banking—or holding company banking—is increasing in Virginia and many bankers believe there will be more important acquisitions by the holding companies in the months ahead.

55 *Ibid.*, July 2, 1961.
56 *Ibid.*, January 14, 1962.
57 Two holding companies were becoming quite active in Virginia. Financial General Corporation was established in Virginia in 1925 under the name of the Morris Plan Corporation of America: this was the original Morris Plan holding company. The First Virginia Corporation was incorporated under the laws of Virginia on October 21, 1949, as Mt. Vernon Insurance Agency, Inc. Its name was changed to the First Virginia Corporation on December 7, 1956.

This growth is occurring while many Virginia banks are in a strait-jacket. The big commercial banks, which are closely associated with the Virginia economy and vital to it, are unable to expand because of the highly restrictive branch banking law in Virginia.[58]

Holding companies were able to pool their lending resources, thereby providing larger lines of credit for the increasing industrial base of the state.

Early in 1961, spurred by competitive pressures and a changing environment, seven banks cooperated in formulating the Virginia Metropolitan Plan. These banks were: First and Merchants National Bank of Richmond, State-Planters Bank of Commerce and Trusts of Richmond, Central National Bank of Richmond, National Bank of Commerce of Norfolk, First National Exchange Bank of Roanoke, Peoples National Bank of Charlottesville, and Shenandoah Valley National Bank.[59] Their plan was to gain the support of other bankers throughout the state for a change in the legislation on branching. They envisioned merger between banks having head offices in metropolitan areas, defined as cities of not less than fifteen thousand.[60] Prior to the convention of the Virginia Bankers Association in June 1961, sponsors of this plan visited bankers throughout the state to generate support for changing the law. Their objective was to gain endorsement of the plan at the convention for subsequent presentation to the General Assembly in January 1962. Small bankers throughout Virginia strongly opposed the plan, however, and its proponents were not optimistic that it would be accepted by the rurally dominated legislature.[61]

[58] Richmond *Times-Dispatch,* November 1, 1961.

[59] Boushall, personal communication, 1968.

[60] This plan, proposing a form of limited branching, indicates a lack of a conceptual scheme of what banking as an industry should be; given a conceptual scheme, implementing legislation should logically follow. The history of the branching issue in Virginia shows no evidence that the concept of what the industry should be was debated; therefore, this approach to the solution of the problem seems to have been overlooked.

[61] One reason for the failure of Virginia bankers to support the plan was advanced by John Green, vice president of First and Merchants, and a member of a group appointed to generate support for the plan throughout the state. The Virginia Metropolitan Plan was primarily sponsored by the large banks in Richmond. To be accepted as a resolution by the Virginia Bankers Association it needed support of the many small banks in the state. This support was hard to gain because the small bankers felt there were inherent dangers in statewide branching systems. Many were reluctant to give up marketing area protection enjoyed under the 1948 legislation, regardless of the broader economic benefits to the state. The sponsoring bankers also did not have sufficient time before the June convention to gather supporters throughout the state.

At the June 1961 meeting of the Virginia Bankers Association, the branching issue was referred for study to a special committee.[62] This committee (the Kramer Committee) was to report its findings to a special convention of the Virginia Bankers Association in November 1961, which would then have brought the branching issue before the 1962 General Assembly. However, this plan was voted down under a motion by Harry Nichols, president of the Southern Bank of Norfolk, and the report was scheduled for the convention the following June. Thus, any action sponsored by the Virginia Bankers Association to ease expansion restrictions would come after the 1962 session of the General Assembly and consequently would be delayed two years, to January 1964, when the Virginia General Assembly would convene again.[63]

Meeting in the late fall and winter of 1961, the Kramer Committee encountered difficulty in obtaining a consensus on recommendations for changes in the legislation on branching. A number of alternatives were considered:

  1. The Virginia Metropolitan Plan
  2. Removal of all legal restrictions on statewide branch banking
  3. Authorization of statewide mergers
  4. Regulation of holding companies under Virginia state law to limit their expansion to the same degree that unit banks were limited; that is, to eliminate the current expansion advantage enjoyed by the holding companies in Virginia

On January 18, 1962, a bill favoring statewide branching was introduced into both houses of the General Assembly. It was a complete surprise to the Virginia banking community, since it came about as the result of the independent action of two legislators, Fred Buck and Shirley T. Holland.[64] Up to this time the

[62] *American Banker*, August 31, 1961. The committee was appointed by the Virginia Bankers Association president, H. E. Wall, and consisted of the following: C. A. Kramer, president, Farmers and Merchants State Bank, Fredericksburg (chairman); R. Cosby Moore, president, National Bank of Commerce, Norfolk; H. Hiter Harris, Jr., president, Southern Bank and Trust, Richmond; Giles H. Miller, Jr., president, First National Bank, Danville; John S. Fulcher, president, Carroll County Bank, Hillsville; Herbert I. Lewis, president, Bank of Gloucester; and Charles C. Abbott, dean of the Graduate School of Business Administration, University of Virginia.

[63] Rather than wait two or more years for possible resolution of the branching issue, the Bank of Virginia formed a holding company as a means of avoiding the expansion restrictions.

[64] Buck represented Abingdon, Virginia, in the House of Delegates. Holland, of Isle of Wight, was chairman of the Senate Committee on Banking and Insurance. Both were presidents of relatively small banks in Virginia. Interviews with several bank officers who were closely involved with the legislation

Kramer Committee had not reached any conclusions or made any report useful to the Virginia Bankers Association. However, on February 1, 1962, the committee recommended that "in the best interest of the public and banking, the Association support legislation which would provide for permissive statewide merger of banks subject to all other restrictions on branches as are now contained in the existing statutes."[65] The recommendation was apparently intended to remove any major opposition to the Buck-Holland bill, which with several amendments became law on July 1, 1962. This legislation opened a new era for banking in Virginia. Virginia bankers interested in statewide expansion could now expand by merger, by holding company, or by a combination of the two methods.

THE 1962–1966 PERIOD OF EXPANSION

1962 legislation. The Virginia Banking Act in 1962 provided an opportunity for statewide expansion of banks. For the first time since 1927 banks could go into any community in Virginia by merger, regardless of population, although additional *de novo* branches could not be established outside the area of the parent bank.

The State Corporation Commission, when satisfied that public convenience and necessity would be served, was permitted to authorize banks having paid-up and unimpaired capital and surplus of $50,000 or more:

1. To branch within the limits of the city, town, or county in which the parent bank was located

2. To branch in cities and counties contiguous to the county or city in which the parent bank was located, provided that branches of a city bank in a contiguous county were not established more than five miles beyond the limits of the city of the parent bank

3. To merge or purchase a bank elsewhere in any other county, city, or town provided that the bank had been in operation for a

---

indicated that Buck and Holland acted on their own, independent of the study being made by the Virginia Bankers Association. In particular, Holland's motivation was said to be based on the recognition of long run needs of the state of Virginia and also of the desirability of giving banks a choice between merger and joining a holding company. Another consideration suggested was that merger provided small bankers with an opportunity to improve their estate liquidity.

[65] Kramer Committee, "Minutes of Meetings of Special Committee on Branch Banking, February 1, 1962."

period of five years or more, except that the State Corporation
Commission under certain conditions could waive this time requirement, provided that branches of a city bank in a contiguous
county were not established more than five miles beyond the limits
of the city of the parent bank[66]

Statewide banking systems. Up to 1962 only one banking organiza-
tion in the state participated in statewide branching. The Bank of
Virginia, with its main office in Richmond, operated branches in
Petersburg, Newport News, Norfolk, Portsmouth, and Roanoke.
The First Virginia Corporation, a bank holding company in
Arlington, and Financial General, a holding company in Washing-
ton, D.C., operated affiliates in several communities in Northern
Virginia.[67]

By the end of 1966 two merged systems and four holding com-
panies were operating in most of the state's metropolitan areas,
regional population centers, and some rural communities. The
banking systems serving these areas are shown in Table A-4,
Appendix A. The six metropolitan areas, with the exception of
Roanoke, were served by at least three systems each; Arlington and
Norfolk were each served by five. One holding company, Virginia
Commonwealth, served all six.[68]

Four secondary population centers—Charlottesville, Danville,
Harrisonburg, and Waynesboro-Staunton, with their surrounding
counties—were not well covered by the large banking systems.
Virginia National Bank operated in all four, but no other system
was active in more than one of these centers. Waynesboro-Staunton
and Augusta County had the most system competition with three.

By 1966 statewide banking systems served areas containing more
than 62.5 percent of Virginia's population of 4,525,976. The six
metropolitan areas contained 56.3 percent; the four regional

[66] See Appendix B, Branching Provisions of the 1962 legislation. A further
change in the 1962 legislation was the fact that public need for additional
banking facilities did not have to be proved on application to the State
Corporation Commission if the proposed new bank were located in a political
subdivision where all banks were owned or controlled by holding companies or
merged systems or both.

[67] Financial General was registered under the federal Investments Act of
1940.

[68] Roanoke and the southwestern region of Virginia, as of the end of 1966,
were also served by the First National Exchange Bank, a large regional banking
system. In August 1967 First National Exchange formed what was then
Virginia's newest holding company—Dominion Bankshares—with Metropolitan
National Bank of Richmond.

population centers, 6.3 percent.[69] The six statewide systems also served many smaller cities, towns, and counties.

The significance of the evolution of statewide systems may be put in better perspective when it is recognized that Virginia is one of only six states where branching is found on an areawide basis:

In discussing the operations of branch banks, it would be most convenient to contrast local branching with branch systems which serve very wide areas. But, unfortunately, for over a century America has had little general experience with even relatively broad branching. In fact, of the 2,797 commercial bank branches, located in counties which were noncontiguous to the head-office county at the end of 1966, four-fifths of them were found in only six states—three adjoining West Coast States: California (47%), Oregon (50%), and Washington (4%), and three adjacent east coast states: North Carolina (14%), South Carolina (5%), and Virginia (5%). On the other hand, there were 33 states which had only ten branches or less in this noncontiguous county category.[70]

Thus, the development of system banking on a statewide basis in Virginia was unique. It was the result of legislation that prohibited *de novo* branches or merger more than five miles into a county contiguous to the expanding bank's home office.[71] The five-mile limit clearly influenced some of the large city banks to expand statewide rather than to serve only their home areas.

It is not clear from the historical record, however. that adequate consideration was given to the advantages of statewide versus regional expansion. In fact, the branching controversy in the Virginia Bankers Association and the clear lack of a plan by any of the interested parties for the development of banking in Virginia, prior to the Buck-Holland bill, suggest that the evolution of Virginia's banking system was more by chance than by design.

Mergers. The trend toward fewer banks in Virginia was accelerated by the wave of mergers after the 1962 legislation. There were seventy mergers between July 1, 1962, and December 31, 1966.[72] These involved one in every four of the 302 banks in Virginia in

[69] Bureau of Population and Economic Research, *Estimates of the Population of Virginia Counties and Cities: July 1, 1967* (Charlottesville, Va.: Graduate School of Business Administration, University of Virginia, August 1967), pp. 1–15.

[70] Fischer, *American Banking Structure,* p. 41.

[71] See Appendix B, Branching Provisions of the 1962 Legislation.

[72] Bureau of Population and Economic Research, "Virginia Banking Survey for Years of 1947, 1961 through 1966," unpublished statistics (Charlottesville, Va.: Graduate School of Business Administration, University of Virginia, 1966).

1962.[73] Thirty different banks were cast in the role of the acquiring bank. Figure I-1 illustrates the increase in such activity after the 1962 legislation.

The decrease in the number of banks would have been greater except for an offsetting increase in the number of new bank formations. During the period 1962–66 thirty-one new banks were established as compared with twenty-one for the previous fourteen-year period. According to the bank executives interviewed, this increase was attributable to the liberal attitude toward bank expansion of the then Comptroller of the Currency (Saxon), the

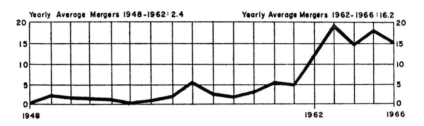

Fig. I-1. Number of commercial bank mergers in Virginia 1948–62. Data from Banking Markets Unit, Division of Research and Statistics, Board of Governors of the Federal Reserve System, *Number of Commercial Banks and Branches by States, FDIC, 1936–1963* (Washington, D.C.: Board of Governors of the Federal Reserve System, 1964), and annual supplements.

need for additional banking facilities in Virginia's fast-growing urban areas, and speculation on bank location in anticipation of a later merger. In addition, twenty-seven holding company acquisitions worked to keep the total number of banks in Virginia higher than it otherwise might have been, since holding company acquisitions continue as separate banks.

Essentially, metropolitan and nonmetropolitan banks were equally active in the role of the acquiring bank. However, three out of four of the banks acquired were in nonmetropolitan areas. Figure I-2 summarizes the merger activity by location.

Statewide merged systems accounted for 30 percent of the mergers; holding companies for 7 percent. Generally, the acquiring bank was considerably larger than the acquired bank, a not unexpected situation since, as was previously noted, three out of four of the acquired banks were in nonmetropolitan areas. Table I-1

[73] *Ibid.*

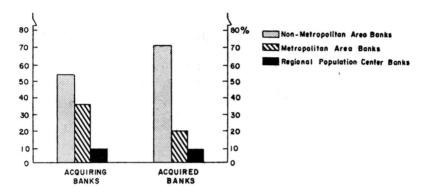

Fig. I-2. Profile of bank mergers by location in Virginia, July 1962 to December 31, 1966. Data from Bureau of Population and Economic Research, "Virginia Banking Survey for Years of 1947, 1961 through 1966," unpublished statistics (Charlottesville, Va.: School of Business Administration, University of Virginia, 1966).

Table I-1. Deposit sizes of merging banks in Virginia, July 1, 1962, to December 31, 1966

	Acquiring bank (millions)	Acquired bank (millions)
Average	$81	$11
Median	$28	$ 8
Range	$1.6 to $536	$.5 to $187

SOURCE: Bureau of Population and Economic Research, "Virginia Banking Survey for Years of 1947, 1961 through 1966," unpublished statistics (Charlottesville, Va.: Graduate School of Business Administration, University of Virginia, 1966).

shows the range, average, and median sizes of the acquiring and acquired banks.

Holding company acquisitions. A comparison of Tables A-5 and A-6 (Appendix A) shows that during the years 1962–66:

1. The number of holding companies doubled.

2. The number of banks affiliated with holding companies grew from nine to thirty-eight.

3. The number of banks affiliated with holding companies increased from 2.9 percent to 15.1 percent of the total number of banks in Virginia.

4. By December 31, 1966, holding company affiliates and their branches accounted for approximately 27 percent of the total banking offices in the state.

5. Between December 31, 1961, and December 31, 1966, holding company deposits, as a percentage of total state deposits, increased from 5.91 percent to 28.11 percent.

Table A-7 (Appendix A) shows that because of the rapid growth of holding companies four were among the ten largest banking organizations in Virginia as of December 31, 1966. These were United Virginia Bankshares Incorporated, Virginia Commonwealth Bankshares, First Virginia Corporation, and Financial General Corporation—in order of size number one, four, five, and seven. Thus, the growth of both holding companies and merged systems

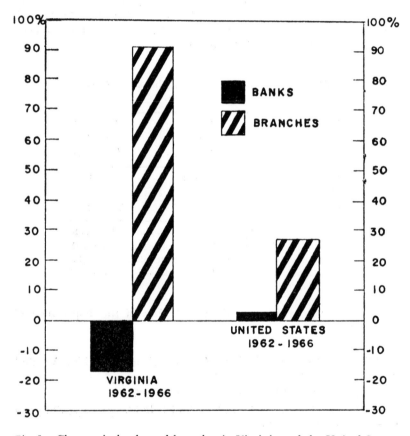

Fig. I-3. Changes in banks and branches in Virginia and the United States, 1962–66. Data from *Number of Commercial Banks and Branches by States, FDIC, 1936–1963* (Washington, D.C.: Board of Governors of the Federal Reserve System 1964), and annual supplements.

into large statewide banking organizations was a unique aspect of the 1962–66 period of banking expansion in Virginia.

Fewer banks and more banking offices. During the years 1962–66 changes in the banking structure in Virginia resulted in a reduction in the number of banks, an increase in the number of branches, and a steady growth in the total number of banking offices. With one exception, these were consistent with the trends in the national banking system. The sole divergence was in the number of banks. Figure I-3 illustrates a decrease in banks of approximately 17 per-cent in Virginia, whereas the number of banks in the United States increased approximately 2½ percent. On the other hand, branches in Virginia increased approximately 91 percent, more than three times the increase in branches for the nation as a whole.

The effect of the 1962 legislation on the rate of change in the number of banks and of branches was substantial. The average rate at which the number of banks decreased was ten times greater for the period 1962–66, compared to the prior fifteen years. The average annual rate at which branches increased was forty-nine per year, compared to eighteen per year for the prior fifteen years, approximately a 2.5-fold increase. Figure I-4 illustrates the trend in banks, branches, and total facilities.

Larger banks. In the late 1950s and early 1960s Virginia bankers saw the need for larger banking organizations with larger lines of

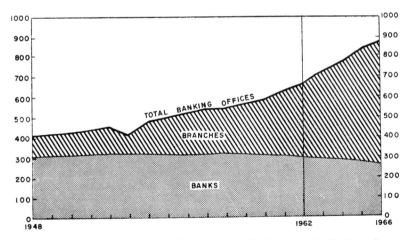

Fig. I-4. Changes in banks and branches in Virginia, 1948–66. Data from *Number of Commercial Banks and Branches by States, FDIC, 1936–1963* (Washington, D.C.: Board of Governors of the Federal Reserve System 1964), and annual supplements.

credit to meet out-of-state competition and to serve better the growing industrial community in Virginia. By 1966 these objectives had been met. The relative size of Virginia's largest banks increased as compared with banks in neighboring states and the District of Columbia. In 1961 no banks in Virginia were among the nation's largest one hundred, but by June 30, 1966, there were two: First and Merchants and Virginia National.[74]

In 1961 North Carolina's Wachovia Bank and Trust Company had deposits approximately 2.8 times larger than First and Merchants, Virginia's largest bank. Washington's Riggs National Bank and Maryland National Bank were 1.9 times larger in terms of deposits. However, by the end of 1966 First and Merchants had gained in deposit size: Wachovia was only 1.8 times larger, Maryland National was 1.5, and Riggs 1.3. Other large banks and banking organizations in Virginia also had gained substantially against their regional competitors by 1966. Bankshares, with deposits of over $640 million, was the largest banking organization in the state.[75]

From 1962 to 1966 deposit concentration among the large banks in Virginia increased. By December 30, 1966, the largest five banks held 36 percent of total state deposits, up from 25 percent five years earlier.[76] Thus, the 1962 legislation reversed a fourteen-year trend toward lower concentration, which had been the consequence of the restrictive legislation enacted in 1948.[77]

Compared with other states, Virginia has a relatively small deposit concentration. In 1965 in California, Rhode Island, New York, and Oregon, what Gerald C. Fischer defines as "large commercial banks" held over 80 percent of each state's deposits, whereas the large banks in Virginia held only 41.9 percent.[78] Though deposit concentration in Virginia is still considerably less than in these other states, a further increase has been viewed by

[74] "300 Largest Commercial Banks in the United States June 30, 1966," *American Banker*, August 1, 1966. First and Merchants ranked eighty-fifth in deposit size; Virginia National, ninetieth.

[75] See Appendix A, Table A-7. Holding companies operating in Virginia at the end of 1966 ranked in size of deposits first, fourth, fifth, and seventh.

[76] See Appendix A, Tables A-2 and A-3.

[77] The Bank of Virginia, said to be the object of the 1948 branching restrictions, grew faster during the period of restricted branching (1948–61) than any of the five larger banks. By the end of 1961, the Bank of Virginia had moved up from sixth to fourth largest in the state. The higher growth rate may be attributed in part to the fact that the 1948 legislation left it with the only branch organization in five of Virginia's six major population centers.

[78] Fischer, *American Banking Structure*, pp. 334–35.

some bankers as a possible constraint on the future growth of banks. Size and concentration, rightly or wrongly, have thus become important considerations for management in planning for expansion.

> Now after a five year wave of mergers and acquisitions Federal regulators seem to be signaling the concentration among larger banks here has gone just about far enough. . . . Most bankers seem resigned to the fact that regulatory authorities will not allow any new formation of banking giants, nor allow any of the big ones now existing to make any really sizable acquisitions. What constituted "giant" or "sizable" are, of course, matters of conjecture. But the interpretation is of considerable interest to bankers here and elsewhere who must try and fathom the Federal Reserve's ruling on "potential competition," a concept first spelled out in a ruling this spring against a new acquisition by a Virginia holding company.[79]

Until after World War II commercial bankers in Virginia were generally not innovators. Throughout this period they tended to maintain the status quo and resist change. In fact, it was the result of external factors (the depression in the 1930s, the Bank Holding Company Act of 1956, competition, and a changing environment in the 1960s) that forced bankers in Virginia away from their traditional posture and into branching and the field of consumer credit. Seemingly, the opportunities for public service and profit were not created by Virginia bankers themselves.

In order to put in proper perspective the conclusion that bankers in Virginia were not innovators until after World War II, it is noted that this same comment was made regarding the banking industry as a whole by George W. Mitchell, a member of the Board of Governors of the Federal Reserve System:

> Some firms and industries have created a product or service, built up public awareness and acceptance for it, and, using generative, adaptive, and innovative forces from within, have established a role and importance for their own enterprise. The result is a *de novo* industrial-commercial business or complex.
>
> Banking is not such an enterprise or industry. It has a pattern of traditional services, an imposed molecular structure, and a pedestrian operating technology, none of which it could call its own. It has not innovated its service products nor shown much adaptive ingenuity in their promotion. Its favorite image has been a passive conformity to the mores of its better customers. Its competitive aggressiveness has been schizophrenic, with large sectors of the industry advocating or supporting

---

[79] *American Banker*, July 24, 1967.

publicly administered price ceilings for time deposits, public prohibitions against the absorption of exchange, and a variety of regulatory devices or postures that by sanction or promise dilute competitive ingenuity.[80]

There is no evidence that commercial bankers, as a group, developed, or desired to develop, a "conceptual scheme" of what the commercial banking industry could or should be. The 1962 legislation was the result of the action of two legislators independent of the Virginia Bankers Association, which at that time was commonly thought to be the authorized channel for the banking industry. This action is further evidence that Virginia bankers were presented with opportunities for profit and growth that they themselves had not created. In fact, had they not been so provincial in 1948, they probably would not have had to reverse their policies in 1962.

A significant aspect of the 1962 legislation was that it worked with the changing economic climate in Virginia, as against the 1948 legislation, which obstructed the oncoming economic developments of the 1950s and early 1960s. One article contends that Virginia banks were now better able to compete with banks in neighboring states for large loans, that more of the state's business could be financed from sources within the state, and that statewide branching produced diversification, greater mobility of funds, and a large number of management personnel with better qualifications and with special skills.[81]

In 1962 the economic pressures finally burst the legislative constraint, which clearly was not in accordance with the needs or desires of the economy of the state. Consequently, several results could be anticipated from the 1962 legislation. In the short run, there would be abnormal or even revolutionary speed in the changes in the banking structure, with a great rush to acquire banks to satisfy a pent-up demand. In the long run, acquisitions would be governed by normal forces of expansion and competition, presumably mostly related to the growth of the state. The advantages and disadvantages of each form of expansion—direct merger and holding company—would not necessarily remain the same in the short run and long run.

[80] George W. Mitchell, "Exogenous Forces in the Development of Our Banking System," *Law and Contemporary Problems*, XXXII (Winter 1967), 3.

[81] Harmon H. Haynes and Charles F. Phillips, Jr., "The Banking Structure of Virginia," *Washington and Lee Law Review*, XXV (Spring 1968), 29–30.

II *Background of the Expansion Decisions*

Prior to passage of the Buck-Holland bill in 1962, both First and Merchants and State-Planters, the lead bank in Bankshares, had been among a group of large Richmond banks actively sponsoring a change in the restrictive 1948 legislation on branching. Together these banks attempted to gain support throughout the state for the Virginia Metropolitan Plan, which would allow the merger of banks in metropolitan areas. The sponsors wanted this plan to be adopted by the Virginia Bankers Association at the June 1961 convention. Had this been done, the Association intended to propose the plan as an amendment to the state banking codes for recommendation to the 1962 General Assembly. The plan, however, was not adopted. Consequently, the management of First and Merchants and of State-Planters assumed that any liberalization of the laws on branching had been delayed for at least another two years; that is, until the next biennial meeting of the General Assembly in 1964. However, the subsequent surprise introduction of the Buck-Holland bill in early 1962 permitted both banks to reconsider their plans.

After the Virginia Metropolitan Plan failed, management at First and Merchants considered expansion by the holding company route. In explaining the sequence of events, an officer of First and Merchants said:

We were actively studying the formation of a holding company and had retained the services of experts in the field. Our planning for a holding company had moved right along, but we feel fortunate, from our standpoint, that the Buck-Holland legislation got into the mill in time for us to take advantage of it. That is to say, we had not gone so far that we could not scrap our plans for a holding company, and embark on a program for expansion by merger, as authorized under the 1962 legislation.

On this same subject, we believe (we do not know) that if some of the others had not gone so far with their commitments for the holding company form, they would have changed their plans, also. But, we feel some had gone so far that they just could not back up and they had to go ahead with their commitments.[1]

[1] John Green, personal communication, 1968.

If it is assumed that direct merger is a better method of expansion, passage of the Buck-Holland bill was an unexpected advantage to First and Merchants, because their competitors supposedly did not have an opportunity to choose the better method. Moreover, if First and Merchants was late in formulating expansion plans by way of the holding company route, the bank was therefore not committed to a less desirable form of expansion when the Buck-Holland bill opened the merger route.

State-Planters reactivated its efforts to form a holding company after the Virginia Metropolitan Plan failed.[2] However, no action resulted until, unexpectedly, in the latter part of 1961, First and Citizens National Bank of Alexandria approached State-Planters with a proposal. By early 1962 four other banks had joined together to form the initial Bankshares group, which commenced operations as a six-bank holding company in January 1963.[3] An officer of Bankshares explained the sequence of events

We knew of the Buck-Holland legislation before we filed with the Securities and Exchange Commission to form United Virginia Bankshares in June, 1962. Therefore, we had the opportunity to drop it and go the merger route if we wanted. But all of the parties had been sold on, and they liked the idea of forming a holding company where everybody would have something to say; we were building something together; all parties were participants. The local autonomy aspect was important, too. No proposal was made to try to force through the merger route. The feeling was just so strong that this was what we wanted to do that this is the way we went.[4]

The original members of Bankshares had the opportunity to change their holding company plans and expand by direct merger under the Buck-Holland legislation, which became effective July 1, 1962. Management was not locked into the holding company form of expansion, even though plans were in the final stages. Furthermore, while it is clear that expansion by holding company was preferred by the Bankshares group and that a participating management philosophy was an essential factor in this decision, it is

---

[2] Lewis B. Flinn, Jr., personal communication, 1968. As early as 1958 the president of State-Planters, J. Harvie Wilkinson, Jr., had considered the concept of formation of a holding company with other large Virginia banks. It was believed this move would improve the competitive position of the banks concerned, regardless of any subsequent action by the state legislators to relax the highly restrictive 1948 branching laws. However, this initial plan for a holding company never got beyond the conceptual state.

[3] See Appendix A, Table A-8.

[4] Flinn, personal communication, 1968.

assumed that had there been sufficient evidence to indicate direct merger was clearly the better route, this path might have been chosen. The decision to expand involved an explicit choice of alternative methods—holding company versus direct merger—as was the case with First and Merchants.

The principal considerations involved in the managements' choices are summarized in the following factor sheets. Each of the factors is examined in subsequent chapters, and an evaluation of the various considerations will be made, using the existing literature on the subject as a point of departure.

EXPANSION BY DIRECT MERGER AS CONSIDERED BY FIRST AND MERCHANTS

The merged form was preferable to the holding company because it provided or permitted:

1. A basis for better organizational control[5]
2. A better solution to the problem of management succession
3. Greater mobility of funds
4. Greater diversification of risk
5. Increased lines of credit to a single customer
6. Greater financial flexibility
7. Larger individual banking units better able to attract industry to Virginia's growing industrial communities
8. Greater community services
9. Certain economies in operation

The merged form was seen to have these disadvantages as contrasted with the holding company:

1. Loss of the merged bank's name
2. Change in the status of the merged bank's board of directors
3. *De novo* branching restrictions in the area of the merged bank

THE ADVANTAGES AND DISADVANTAGES OF EXPANSION BY HOLDING COMPANY AS CONSIDERED BY BANKSHARES

The holding company form was preferable to the merged form because it provided or permitted:

[5] The order of the factors on these sheets does not indicate priority.

1. Greater *de novo* branching opportunities
2. Efficiency equal to the merged form
3. Flexibility in raising capital
4. Greater flexibility in expansion
5. Local autonomy for affiliates
6. Local identity for affiliates
7. Decentralized decision-making provides more flexibility and opportunity to management
8. Lower effective reserve ratio on system deposits

The holding company form was seen to have these disadvantages as contrasted to the merged form:

1. Complications due to Securities and Exchange Commission regulations
2. A more complex organization
3. Complications from regulations by more than one agency
4. Lack of a single corporate image

Both forms were preferable to an individual bank in Virginia because they provided or permitted:

1. Increased organization size to attract and train management personnel
2. A solution to a management succession problem
3. Certain economic benefits to the acquired bank stockholders
4. Greater credit and funds mobility
5. Expanded services, such as data processing, trusts

KEY EXPANSION STRATEGY, FIRST AND MERCHANTS

1. To merge only into areas where the growth rate will keep pace with or exceed the system as a whole
2. To avoid dilution of book value and earnings but to give "fair value"
3. To keep strategy flexible because of possible difficulty with future mergers owing to increasing competition for the remaining banks and the attitude of the regulatory agencies
4. To offset *de novo* branching restrictions in the area of the merged bank by acquiring banks already having branch offices
5. To offset the loss of the merged bank's board of directors by appointing an area advisory board

Key Expansion Strategy, Bankshares

1. To expand in growth areas, with emphasis on the Virginia urban corridor from Washington, D.C., south to Richmond and east through Williamsburg, Newport News, and Norfolk

2. To acquire a leading bank in an area, if possible a bank with deposits of over $10 million

3. To emphasize local autonomy through a decentralized management philosophy

4. To deal directly with and through the management and not the shareholders of prospective affiliates

III *Operational and Organizational Considerations*

LITERATURE

IN the literature, operational and organizational characteristics of holding companies and merged systems are usually discussed with regard to the production functions of a bank. Comparisons are commonly made between a holding company and a unit bank, or between a merged system and a unit bank. There are relatively few direct and comprehensive comparisons of the characteristics of the two forms.[1] For this reason, numerous advantages are cited as common to both forms of organization, on the basis of a comparison of each to a common standard—a unit bank.

The general opinion is that there are benefits from economies of scale both in holding companies and in merged banking organizations.[2] (Economies of scale are reductions in the cost of various functions—such as loans and checking accounts—as the number of units increases.) One statement on which most commentators agree is that the close integration of the typical branch operation makes possible greater economies than does a holding company.[3] Yet holding companies having affiliates with a large branch system apparently might achieve economies comparable with those of merged systems of similar size.

Research in economies of scale includes size-to-output studies

---

[1] An exception to this finding is Lewis B. Flinn, Jr., "Holding Company versus Branch Banking in Virginia" (Thesis, The Stonier Graduate School of Banking, Rutgers University, 1967).

[2] Gerald C. Fischer, *Bank Holding Companies* (New York: Columbia University Press, 1961), pp. 87, 119, 128; Palmer T. Hogenson, *The Economies of Group Banking* (Washington, D.C.: Public Affairs Press, 1955), pp. 142–43; Frederick W. Bell and Neil B. Murphy, "Returns to Scale in Commercial Banking," *Bank Structure and Competition* (Chicago: Federal Reserve Bank of Chicago, 1967), pp. 118–76; Federal Reserve Bank of Boston, "Economies of Scale in Commercial Banking," *Business Review*, March 1967, pp. 3–11; *ibid.*, April 1967, pp. 2–10; *ibid.*, June 1967, pp. 13–19; *ibid.*, July 1967, pp. 12–19; David A. Alhadeff, *Monopoly and Competition in Banking* (Berkeley: University of California Press, 1954), chapter VI; George J. Benston, "Branch Banking and Economics of Scale," *Journal of Finance*, XX (May 1965), 312–31.

[3] W. Ralph Lamb, *Group Banking: A Form of Banking Concentration and Control in the United States* (New Brunswick, N.J.: Rutgers University Press, 1962), pp. 236–37.

and size-to-performance variable studies.[4] Findings in each category generally support the view that economies of scale do exist. The validity of size-to-output studies suffers from the failure to measure bank output with a common yardstick. According to a survey of banking research, conflicting results, inadequate data, and imperfect methodology make it difficult to determine what size bank is most efficient.[5] In all probability, economies of scale "will depend on the composition of the services rendered so that at best there may be only an optimal distribution of size of banks rather than a single optimal size."[6]

One conflicting piece of evidence is that diseconomies tend to offset any economies of scale, which in the branch structure might be less important than diseconomies; therefore, branching cannot be supported solely on a cost-advantage basis.[7] However, a later study reports that diseconomies in branching could be overcome by growth as long as fairly wide branching was permitted, perhaps on a statewide basis.[8]

Research findings in size-to-performance variable studies also support economies of scale. Larger banks are said to have higher earnings in proportion to assets and capital, even though they tend to pay higher average rates on savings, charge lower average rates on loans, and have a higher ratio of time deposits to total deposits. Also, economies of scale in group banking are supported by evidence that "their rate of return on total capital funds for 1957 was 10 percent higher than the reported net profits for all commercial banks."[9] Nevertheless, findings regarding size-to-performance variables are said to be biased in that the greater earnings of larger banks result, in part, from the different nature of their operations without regard to scale.[10] For instance, larger

[4] Size-to-output studies relate to output in terms of the production functions of banks—loans, checking accounts, savings accounts. Size-to-performance variables relate to performance variables in terms of commonly used measures of bank operating performance, such as ratio of earnings to assets.

[5] Federal Reserve Bank of Chicago, "Competition in Banking: What Is Known? What Is the Evidence?" *Business Conditions,* February 1967, pp. 7–16.

[6] *Ibid.,* p. 15.

[7] Paul M. Horvitz, "Economies of Scale in Banking," *Private Financial Institutions* (Englewood Cliffs, N.J.: Prentice-Hall, 1963), pp. 1–54; Benston, pp. 312–31.

[8] Paul M. Horvitz and Bernard Shull, "The Impact of Branch Banking on Bank Performance," in *Studies in Banking Competition and the Banking Structure* (Washington, D.C.: Comptroller of the Currency, 1966), pp. 141–86.

[9] Lamb, p. 236.

[10] Federal Reserve Bank of Chicago, "Competition in Banking: What Is Known? What Is the Evidence?" p. 15.

banks may serve large commercial accounts with smaller administrative unit costs.

The weight of the evidence suggests that economies of scale exist in large banks of both forms, although they may be greater in branch systems because closer integration of operation is possible. For example, trust departments and loan and investment portfolios in holding company affiliates cannot be integrated, and holding company affiliates cannot obtain comparable integration in the area of checking accounts because they remain separate banks. However, measurement of this apparent advantage is difficult, if not impossible, given the limitations of current research methodology.

The consensus is that certain organizational characteristics of both holding companies and merged systems facilitate efficiency in operations.[11] Some efficiencies are specifically attributed to centralization and specialization, others to greater organizational flexibility.[12] However, there is no clear evidence of the relative importance of these contributing factors.

Operating efficiencies stem from centralization of certain activities.[13] Centralized purchasing of supplies and equipment, both consumables and capital items, may result in greater quantity discounts and lower administrative cost per unit of purchase. Economies may also result from centralization of such services as auditing, legal counsel, accounting, tax assistance, operations assistance, and advertising. Tangible and measurable efficiencies are deemed possible in both holding companies and merged systems in contrast with unit banks. However, in merged systems centralization of functions that cannot be combined in holding companies may lead to even greater economies.

An often-cited advantage of both forms of expansion is that the large organization is better able than the small unit bank to attract and hold superior managerial talent. With a few exceptions, this advantage is discussed in the context of banking's acute problem of management succession. It is argued that of all of the difficulties facing bank management in the United States today, the personnel

[11] Robert J. Lawrence, *The Performance of Bank Holding Companies* (Washington, D.C.: Board of Governors of the Federal Reserve System, June 1967), pp. 5–6; Marcus Nadler and Jules I. Bogen, *The Bank Holding Company* (New York University: Graduate School of Business Administration, 1959), pp. 18–19, 24–29; Federal Reserve Bank of Boston, "Economies of Scale," *Business Review*, March, April, June, July, 1967.

[12] In this sense efficiency stems from centralization and specialization as opposed to economies of scale; an organization can achieve benefits from these factors without an increase in the size of its operations.

[13] Hogenson, p. 143; Nadler and Bogen, p. 24.

problem is one of the most significant. According to the president of the Federal Reserve Bank of Philadelphia, the failure of bankers to prepare young men for succession is a prime reason for bank mergers.[14] In coping with this problem, large banks of both forms benefit from their superior managerial drawing power, which is generally attributed to more opportunities for advancement, more job responsibilities, better salary scales, and wider benefits. Also, they have a greater capability for employing legal, tax, and other specialists. However, neither form of expansion is regarded as superior with respect to hiring and holding first-class managerial talent and specialists.

Another widely cited advantage of both holding companies and merged systems is that the large banking organization has superior opportunities to extend services and special skills throughout all units of the organization. Ordinarily cited are: auditing, appraising, investment counseling, safe deposit, trust, legal, accounting, purchasing, research, credit, and tax services, employee compensation and benefit plans, and institutional advertising.[15] Furthermore, the potential of holding companies for organizing the production of banking services is said to be greater than that of independent banks; that is, the produce-versus-buy alternative gives them greater flexibility.[16] An affiliate may produce its own banking services or buy from the lead bank in the holding company, from a nonbanking subsidiary of the holding company, or from a nonaffiliated bank. Here again, however, there is no basis for concluding that either form is better able to extend specialized services throughout its system.

An important, but less widely discussed, advantage is that units in both forms may benefit from the successes and mistakes of other units.[17] Executives throughout a system have opportunities to exchange ideas and discuss common problems. The result is a beneficial cross-fertilization of ideas concerning operating improvements as well as solutions to general operating problems. Also, the audit of operating units by a holding company, lead bank, or home office is often said to contribute to operating efficiencies.[18] Through internal-performance evaluation, similar units may be compared and management encouraged to improve the operations. The less active or progressive banks or branches may be identified

[14] Fischer, *Bank Holding Companies*, p. 96.
[15] *Ibid.*, p. 87; Nadler and Bogen, p. 24.
[16] Lawrence, p. 5.
[17] Fisher, *Bank Holding Companies*, p. 87.
[18] Hogenson, p. 140.

and perhaps moved along at a faster and more efficient pace. Holding companies and merged systems are regarded as equally capable of sharing operating improvements.

A fundamental difference between holding companies and merged systems is alleged to exist in the area of management control. This difference stems from the special relationship between holding companies and their affiliates. "By its very nature, this parent-subsidiary relation can exist only in holding company banking and not in either unit or branch banking."[19] Each affiliate in a holding company system retains independent bank status with a board of directors and a president. In contrast, a branch system has only one board of directors and one president for the entire system and does not face the problem of minority interests in units throughout the system.

The argument that the holding company has a basic advantage in its decentralized corporate structure is countered by the view that merged systems may also make effective use of decentralization. Research indicates that effective use of decentralization in merged systems is possible and desirable.[20] A study of this issue concludes that good organization is essential to good management, that behind an organization there must be a philosophy of management, and that management must choose and balance the advantages and disadvantages of centralization versus decentralization; but that decentralization is the better way to organize because it stimulates managers, gets better results, and develops initiative and creativity. Nevertheless, it is argued that holding companies have greater opportunities to decentralize management than is possible in branch systems, where the tendency is to concentrate authority in the head office.[21] However, management organization and policies may minimize the effects of this basic characteristic when centralized management control restricts the operational autonomy of affiliates.[22] On the other hand, a high degree of decentralization is possible where the affiliates have broad policy and operating responsibilities.

Group banking permits a wide variety of organization patterns since each affiliated bank must have its own board of directors and officers who are

19 Nadler and Bogen, p. 21.
20 Michael J. Schmitz, "Centralization versus Decentralization in a Branch Banking Organization" (Thesis, The Stonier Graduate School of Banking, Rutgers University, 1964).
21 Flinn, pp. 77, 82.
22 Nadler and Bogen, pp. 30–31. The authors also observe that decentralization is a dominant trend in business management today (p. 23).

charged by law with the responsibility for operating their own banks. As a result, the member banks may be run as independent institutions, policies may be set through consultation with the holding company management or the parent's officers may exert a very large measure of influence over management of the subsidiary.[23]

On the basis of the literature, the independent corporate structure of the holding company assures, at least in theory, more autonomy for its affiliates than does the merged organization for its branches.

RESEARCH FINDINGS

Management Effectiveness

The critical issue regarding management effectiveness in the banks studied concerned the question: Does a particular form of corporate organization lead to, or result in, more effective management? This question was answered in the affirmative by both First and Merchants and Bankshares, even though the two banks chose different forms of organization. The arguments centered on points involving organization theory—centralization versus decentralization, and local autonomy versus a more direct form of management control.

The management of First and Merchants preferred the less complex corporate structure of the merged form as providing a basis for better control and, consequently, greater unity of purpose.[24] They believed there was less potential for the development of problems in policy formulation and execution since the merged form had one board of directors and one senior management group. They felt that the unity necessary to the effective operation of a large banking organization was harder to achieve in a holding company comprised of a number of separate banks, each with its own board of directors and senior management legally responsible for the soundness of planning and operations.

Another aspect of control cited by First and Merchants was that one senior management group carrying out the policies of a single board tended to reduce the time and effort required of management at the local level. Local management, therefore, could devote more time to business development and customer service.

[23] *Ibid.*, p. 31.
[24] John Green, personal communication, 1968.

Bankshares preferred the holding company form because it provided more local autonomy.[25] Thus, this form was suitable for implementation of Bankshares' management philosophy, which was based on the idea of a participatory enterprise. Each of the six original affiliates was represented on Bankshares' board of directors. Although new affiliates were not necessarily represented, a committee of presidents was devised for the establishment of certain policies.

We try to get together at least once a month with the presidents committee and talk about problems, policies, and new services that Bankshares should provide. Thus, we have a joint effort: (1) to become a statewide organization, (2) to build a larger organization to make bigger loans to Virginia businesses, (3) to extend new services throughout the system, and (4) by pooling resources to provide special services, such as in the computer area, of a quality no one bank could afford.[26]

Bankshares' management believed that greater local automomy through participatory management was an important factor in attracting new affiliates. Even so, they found it difficult to convince some bankers interested in joining a holding company that what they said about their method of operation was true. Some had heard discouraging reports from those who had joined other holding companies. Nevertheless, Bankshares' cooperative management philosophy was an attractive element of their expansion strategy.[27] One officer of Bankshares observed that local autonomy was particularly important to the executive operating a well-managed, profitable bank; he was generally thought to be a strong individual who did not want to give up any measure of operating responsibility.

Banks interested in joining Bankshares were told that the holding company retained central direction in changes in the top two management positions and their salaries and in the purchase of fixed assets and lease of new offices. Affiliates were authorized to spend up to their depreciation for new assets, but anything more required approval by the holding company. In this way the control of real estate and the purchase of major assets throughout the system were coordinated. During the years 1962–66, $12.5 million was raised to meet affiliates' plans for major building programs. Dividend policy and matters that could result in conflicts of interest were other areas where the holding company retained central direction.

[25] Lewis B. Flinn, Jr., personal communication, 1968.
[26] *Ibid.*   [27] *Ibid.*

Bankshares' position was that the decentralized nature of the holding company offered greater flexibility and opportunities for management than the typical branch system.[28] This aspect of holding company operations was thought to be inherently attractive, offering a superior environment for developing successors within the industry. The most important aspect of its decentralized management concept was the legal status of each affiliate's board of directors.[29] Individual affiliate boards were thought to be a very real force in promoting and maintaining decentralization of management by providing more interest in management and market development at the local level.

Bankshares recognized that the merged form had a simple corporate structure, one board of directors, and one senior management group.[30] One officer said that the less complex structure of the merged system simplified policy formulation and execution. Problems of diffused authority, internal conflict at the management level, and administrative complications (that is, separate records for each affiliate) were thought to be more easily avoided in the merged system.

However, Bankshares contended that these problems could be overcome since the holding company provided substantially the same range of management control options as the merged system. Furthermore, Bankshares believed that the administrative problems of the holding company were compensated for by the definite advantages of more aggressive and responsive affiliates.

The positions of First and Merchants and of Bankshares suggest that there is a direct and important relationship between the form of corporate organization and the effectiveness of management. However, when their views are examined, it is clear that they do not settle issues involving questions of organization theory, of the role of the formal and informal organization, or of the attitudes and opinions of management. Consequently, it is difficult to decide in favor of either form. The answer may be that one form is better, or worse, for a particular group depending on the general outlook of that group. In this context, the positions of both parties generate

[28] *Ibid.*
[29] "Legal status" of the board of directors refers to the responsibilities of bank directors specified in banking statutes. Article 6 of the *Laws of Virginia Relating to Banking and Finance* states: "The affairs of every bank or banking institution incorporated under the laws of this state shall be managed by a board of directors which shall consist of not less than five persons" (sec. 6.1–45).
[30] Flinn, personal communication, 1968.

several points concerning the selection of a corporate form for expansion. Obviously, different methods of organizing and managing banking groups may be employed regardless of the corporate form; both merged systems and holding companies may be either highly centralized or highly decentralized. Therefore, differences in organizational structure and management control seem to be a function of the attitudes of individual managements and to depend in part on the individual situation.

Both managements admit that there is increased potential for administrative conflict in the holding company, because of the voting control and the role of the directors in holding company affiliates. On this issue it is argued that control in the holding company is in fact less absolute because affiliate management has more autonomy than lower level management in a merged system. The legal responsibilities of affiliate directors and the different voting control situations that may exist in holding company affiliates account for this conclusion.

In general, four different voting control situations may exist in a holding company, whereas there is only one in the merged system. A holding company may have complete control (100 percent), very large control (80 to 99 percent), bare majority control (perhaps 51 percent), or minority control (less than 50 percent). The implication for affiliate directors is different in each of these situations. Directors are responsible to *all* stockholders, minority as well as majority, and they have to consider different factors in each case. Questions of policy, such as affiliate dividends, may have a different meaning to the holding company as a shareholder and to the individual investor as a shareholder. Individuals may desire a high dividend payout for income, whereas the holding company may desire a low payout in the light of provisions for capital growth and expansion. Various kinds of capital expenditures— for example, purchase of real estate—may also be viewed differently. Clearly, the resolution of such policy issues may, and probably will, depend on the voting control situation in each affiliate.

When the holding company votes all, or almost all, of the shares of the affiliate, policy conflict is probably no worse a problem than in the merged form; that is, equivalent "power to remove and replace" rests with the parent.[31] However, the holding company does not have the same power in the other three voting control

---

[31] As noted in its *Annual Report* for 1967, Bankshares owns 96.4 percent or more of each of its affiliates, and two of the nine are 100-percent owned.

situations, because management must accommodate satisfactorily the minority interest, no matter how small. Furthermore, the holding company has to replace directors at the affiliate level, and there is no guarantee that the views of new directors with regard to policy will conform to those of the old, a problem that does not arise in the merged organization.

Another important difference between the two forms is the possibility of having many boards of directors in a holding company as opposed to one in a merged system. This has distinct implications for control; for example, the comment that "no bank holding company can exert a veto power over actions of the board of directors of bank subsidiaries" takes on specific meaning.[32] In this case the chief officer of one large Virginia holding company described control as more a "sell" than a "tell" proposition, whereas in the merged system the control may be much more direct. The difference is illustrated in the situation where the affiliate board will not relieve an ineffective president of his duties. Assuming the holding company has voting control, a meeting of its stockholders could be called to vote in new affiliate directors who would discharge the president. However, this action would be unusual, as it probably would cause problems in community relations or business development if the dismissed directors were influential in the community. Similar problems could arise from the removal of a branch manager in a merged system, but the potential consequences probably would not be so severe. For this reason, in the opinion of the aforementioned chief officer, the holding company may have to put up with poor management longer than the merged form. Not only is control of management at the affiliate level less direct, but the time required to obtain the desired response may also be commensurately longer.

Several points regarding Bankshares' implementation of local autonomy are significant: six original affiliates were represented on Bankshares' board of directors; new affiliates were not necessarily represented; and a committee of presidents was devised for establishment of certain policies. This pattern established the character of local autonomy in the Bankshares organization, particularly for those initial affiliate officers who are also members of the holding company board. Autonomy for these affiliates is preserved as long as they serve in their original roles. However, their successors may be more readily controlled. New presidents and directors may, and probably will, come from within the established organization.

---

[32] Nadler and Bogen, p. 22.

Consequently, the succeeding generations of management will tend to be system oriented rather than unit-bank oriented, and as a result, differences in control between the two forms will tend to narrow, although not disappear, over time.

It is difficult to generalize regarding the time either form provides local management to devote to operations as opposed to considerations of policy. In both forms the amount of time management may devote to business development and customer service at the local level seems to depend on the range and depth of services provided and the type of control exercised by the parent organization. For example, a holding company with a high degree of centralized management control and a large service organization may provide management at the affiliate level with as much time to devote to business development and customer service as a merged system.

Management Succession

Both Bankshares and First and Merchants contended that their respective forms of organization improved their ability to compete for and retain management talent and to solve the problem of management succession. According to Bankshares, this benefit was shared by both forms as the result of the increase in organization size. On the other hand, First and Merchants contended that the merged system benefited more than the holding company.

First and Merchants preferred the merged form because only one organization was involved in expansion. Their position was that fewer personnel were required at the policy development and operating levels, whereas each holding company affiliate had a continuing need for management at all levels as long as it remained an individual bank. One officer of First and Merchants expressed the opinion that merger tended to make allocation of these resources more effective.[33]

First and Merchants favored direct merger also because it resulted in larger individual banking units thought to be more attractive to the young person in view of greater opportunities, salaries, and responsibilities. Furthermore, their experience indicated management personnel in larger organizations typically were more willing to accept assignments in less desirable locations because such assignments were viewed as training grounds or stepping stones to bigger things, and not as lifetime jobs.

[33] Green, personal communication, 1968.

The importance of this point was illustrated by the statement made to an officer of First and Merchants by the chief officer of an independent bank in an outlying area:

How can I conceivably attract anybody to come here and live? As far as profits of the banks are concerned and because of lack of loan demand it is difficult to pay a beginning salary to attract good young management. And, furthermore, what is really available here in the community to attract permanent management? There is nothing here, except what has existed back through the century. Young qualified and educated people are interested in going where they can grow and where they do not have a definite ceiling placed on their abilities. They do not want to come here.[34]

First and Merchants preferred the merged form because it was thought to provide greater flexibility for the movement of management personnel. Transfer was a matter internal to one organization in the eyes of the personnel committee, the president, and the board of directors. In contrast, a transfer in a holding company was seen by First and Merchants as having the possibility of complications because it involved two or more separate banks, each responsible for maintaining and managing its own resources. Consequently, a conflict of interest between two corporate entities and two boards of directors might result. For this reason, according to an officer of First and Merchants, movement of personnel was easier in the merged system, and the holding company could not possibly achieve this flexibility.

In the view of Bankshares' management, increased size gave both forms an advantage relative to an individual bank in Virginia in competing for and holding management talent.[35] Large organizations had the staff for training recruits to the banking industry, and employee benefits were superior to those provided by small banks. However, Bankshares argued that the holding company offered more top executive positions than a branch organization of comparable size, since each affiliate has a president.

Bankshares cited as an advantage of both forms over an individual bank in Virginia the fact that both provided a solution to the problem of management succession.[36] In fact, three of the banks that joined Bankshares had a management succession problem, and most banks that approached Bankshares on an unsolicited

---

[34] *Ibid.* In this opinion there are numerous implicit assumptions about the community and "young people" that may not be valid. The opinion, however, is thought to be both honest and informed.

[35] Flinn, personal communication, 1968.

[36] *Ibid.*

basis had the same problem. Each of the three banks was supplied a new president from within the system.

According to the literature, large banks typically are superior to small banks in attracting and keeping management talent: "As is true of any of the larger enterprises, there are more and varied opportunities for able individuals interested in banking as a career with a group of banks, than within a single unit."[37] Larger institutions have higher salaries and more extensive employee benefits and training and educational programs as added incentives for employment. Thus, the literature supports the position that these benefits are attributable to increased size rather than to the type of organization.

In Virginia, where holding companies and merged systems are actively competing in major markets throughout the state, neither appears to have an advantage on the issue of employee benefits. The following factor sheet shows that employee programs are generally alike in holding companies and merged systems.

EMPLOYEE BENEFITS AND PROGRAMS
COMMON TO ONE OR MORE
OF THE MERGED SYSTEMS
AND HOLDING COMPANIES
IN VIRGINIA

Retirement plan[38]
Group life insurance plan
Hospitalization and major medical plan
Profit sharing plan (officers and staff)
Employee training programs
Personnel department
Centralized recruitment
Employee education programs

In one aspect of employee benefits, however, there may be a difference between the two forms. After a merger, the corporate benefit plan automatically extends to the new employees. But after a holding company acquisition, the benefit plan for the group is

[37] Hogenson, p. 143.
[38] Data from 1962–66 *Annual Reports* of First Virginia Corporation, First and Merchants National Bank, Virginia Commonwealth Bankshares, Virginia National Bank, and United Virginia Bankshares Incorporated.

not required to cover the new affiliate. One study found uniform plans and fringe benefits in only half of the holding companies surveyed.[39]

First and Merchants' argument that greater flexibility in movement of personnel is a benefit of the merged form is probably valid. Although it is difficult to generalize about the issue of flexibility of movement, control of personnel is thought to be easier in the merged form because it is more difficult to order changes in the holding company. The matter of moving management personnel is obviously internal to the merged organization, while changes in holding company management involve different corporate organizations. According to the chief officer of the lead bank of a Virginia holding company, which also has some branches, it makes a great deal of difference whether he is dealing with one of his branch managers or with the president of an affiliate. The latter situation, he said, involves a greater risk of administrative conflict, since a matter such as movement of a key manager in an affiliate required "selling"; in a branch the change could be "directed."

Both forms of organizations, when they have centralized recruiting and training and benefit plans, can achieve flexibility in movement of personnel, particularly when their efforts are specifically aimed at solving the problem of management succession. Bankshares quickly and without difficulty provided top management from within its organization for three of the banks that joined.[40] Movement of management in a holding company has the same benefit First and Merchants alleged for a merged system. An assignment is not necessarily a lifetime job: it may be the stepping-stone to jobs of greater responsibility. However, the concept of local autonomy in the holding company form seems to increase the likelihood of a bank officer's remaining in one location because of implications regarding his motivation, the importance of the community, and his interests in community affairs.

First and Merchants' position that the merged form requires fewer personnel at the policy development and operating level would appear to be valid for several reasons. First, in deposit and trust areas, where a merged system can integrate operations and a holding company cannot, there may be savings of both management and staff through the consolidation of functions. Second, a merged system needs fewer directors since holding company affiliates are legally required to have boards in each of their

[39] Fischer, *Bank Holding Companies*, pp. 87 ff.
[40] Flinn, personal communication, 1968.

separate banks. Third, lesser management skills may be needed to fill the top position in a branch than in a holding company affiliate of comparable size and functions, as the past chief officer of both a holding company and a large bank in Virginia has argued. The affiliate president has to deal with his board of directors as well as with the community; the reputation of the bank largely depends on his performance. In contrast, a branch manager, in this officer's experience, benefits from the "marketing image and reputation" of the home office, making his administrative and marketing problems less complex. If this argument is valid, a merged system can operate offices of comparable size with a lower order of managerial skill. Consequently, it may be easier to fill the management needs of a merged system than of a holding company.

Both forms, when compared with a unit bank, may save on officers and employees in staffing for limited banking services in branches throughout the systems. Only deposit facilities may be needed in certain locations because it is unnecessary to erect expensive buildings for each office. Additionally, through centralization of some functions, full banking services can be offered areas which could not support even a small unit bank offering limited services.[41]

Several other factors affect the efficient use of personnel in both types of systems when compared with a unit bank. First, the experiences of the organizations studied suggest that there is a tendency for expanding systems to upgrade and broaden the scope of services in a new marketing area. Such expansion may more than offset any savings in personnel that might otherwise benefit the organization in aggregate. Also, this study shows that acquisition does not necessarily result in a reduction of personnel; that is, corporate policy may dictate that excess personnel be retained, and that attrition reduce the staff over the long run.[42]

Operating Economies

As suggested by the literature, large banks, whether holding companies or merged systems, clearly ought to be able to achieve more operating economies than smaller unit banks. The critical question, however, is which of the two forms can achieve greater operating economies? On this issue, both First and Merchants and

[41] Federal Reserve Bank of Richmond, "The New Look in Banking Structure," *Monthly Review*, July 1963, p. 3.
[42] Green, personal communication, 1968.

Bankshares cited operating economies as an advantage of their respective form of organization.

First and Merchants preferred the merged form since it led to operating economies in such areas as purchasing, insurance, data processing, and personnel administration, although it was acknowledged that economies in these areas could be offset by the cost of new services, improved quality of existing services, and other factors.[43] Smaller banks could usually be integrated into the system with greater ease. Merging a larger bank tended to lead to problems involving consolidation of functions and personnel normally centralized in the home office. On this subject a First and Merchants officer said:

> Let me say that the hoped-for economies have not been as realistic as we had thought they would be, and we have not experienced them yet. We hope to in the future, but I think we would make a very serious mistake if we tried to achieve economies through a negative approach. I consider reducing the merged staff by arbitrary laying-off or just saying you do not have a job because we eliminated your position to be a terrible mistake to make at the local scene.
>
> In no case have we dispensed with personnel services as a result of merger. Normal attrition has taken care of this problem. That has been a policy long before the passage of the merger law.[44]

Bankshares' position was that both forms shared many of the advantages attributed to large banking units: centralization of support functions (purchasing and system advertising) and use of specialists for trust, legal, tax, accounting, data processing, and other services.[45] The merits of one form as compared with the other were described by an officer of Bankshares in these terms:

> My feeling is that selection of an organizational form will in time (perhaps not initially) be primarily a matter of economics. That is to say initially the selection of an organization form may be based on evaluation of factors (i.e., legislative) then existing, but in the final analysis the choice will be proven out by economics. For example, if a holding company cannot operate just as effectively and efficiently as a branch system, then there is no reason not to make the holding company one merged institution (assuming this is feasible as it is in Virginia).[46]

Bankshares thought that its own experiences and the growth of holding companies in Virginia and elsewhere suggested that the holding company form was generally competitive with merged systems; if not, other factors, such as the *de novo* branching ad-

[43] *Ibid.*   [44] *Ibid.*
[45] Flinn, personal communication, 1968.   [46] *Ibid.*

vantage in Virginia, tended to offset any operational inefficiencies. Big banks of both forms ought to benefit from economies of scale over small unit banks:

Empirical studies of this issue . . . are subject to both conceptual and methodological difficulties . . . but they suggest that (a) there are significant economies of scale in banking (i.e., costs per unit of output decline as size increases) as bank size increases up to $10,000,000 in deposits and there may be some less significant economies beyond that size; . . . (b) branch banks tend to have higher total costs than unit banks of equal deposit size . . . but differences in costs between branch and unit operations decrease rapidly, as size increases; . . . and (c) it is doubtful that a holding company can achieve the same economies of operation as a branch system.[47]

However, the answer to the question of whether a holding company or a merged system can achieve greater economies of operations is not clear from either the literature or the experiences of the organizations studied.

The merged form has one advantage over the holding company, but the extent of this advantage largely depends on the objectives and policies of a particular management group and not on universally valid standards. Greater economies are theoretically possible in a merged system because some operating functions cannot be combined in a holding company—the corporate entity of each affiliate requires that trust accounts and bond and loan portfolios be separately maintained. Consequently, it appears that a merged system has the potential for a somewhat greater degree of economy than a holding company:

Most commentators on banking concentration agree that the close integration typical of branch systems makes greater economies possible than those achieved in holding company banking. It should be pointed out, however, that many of the large group systems make extensive use of branch offices in those locations where they are permitted by law.[48]

Assuming that the organizations studied are comparable in all other areas affecting profitability, the data in Table III-1 suggest that the type of corporate organization is a matter of indifference in Virginia when measured by two broad indicators of operating efficiency: earnings on deposits and earnings on capital.[49]

---

[47] Harmon H. Haynes and Charles F. Phillips, Jr., "The Banking Structure of Virginia," *Washington and Lee Law Review,* XXV (Spring 1968) , p. 30.

[48] Lamb, pp. 236–37.

[49] A statistical comparison of the average of the ratios of five-year earnings to deposits shows a *t* value of .10, and a comparison of the average of the

Table III-1. Ratios of net operating earnings to total deposits and to capital, 1962–66

	Bankshares		First and Merchants	
Year	Earnings/ deposits	Earnings/ capital	Earnings/ deposits	Earnings/ capital
1962	.89	9.3	.97	10.2
1963	.88	9.9	.91	9.4
1964	.98	12.6	.99	10.4
1965	.97	12.2	.99	11.2
1966	1.03	13.1	1.10	12.6
Average	.95	11.42	.992	10.76

SOURCES: United Virginia Bankshares 1967 *Annual Report* (for 1963–66); secretary treasurer of United Virginia Bankshares (for 1962); First and Merchants National Bank *Annual Report*, 1962–66. See also Appendix A, Table A-2, A-3.

NOTE: 1962 data for Bankshares are on a *pro forma* basis for the original six members.

Ultimately, the choice is between two positions: (1) that the merged form can be more efficient because of closer integration in areas such as trust, loan, and investment portfolios; (2) that there is no significant difference between the forms as suggested by the profitability experiences of the organizations studied. Because the validity of the quantitative comparison is limited by its constraining assumptions, small sample size, and short period of measurement, the better choice is the first.[50]

The relative efficiency of the two forms, however, also depends on the objectives and policies of the individual management group. Management decisions on the extent of centralization or decentralization will affect integration at all levels of the organization.[51] This relationship is shown in Figures III-1 and III-2.

ratios of five-year earnings to capital shows a *t* value of .68. With 8 degrees of freedom, a *t* value as large as 2.306 would occur by chance alone with a probability of .95 when the samples are from the same distribution. These data, therefore, do not support the hypothesis that the samples are from different populations.

[50] Many factors apart from the type of organization could contribute to differences in profitability. Consequently, valid research results require answers to such questions as: What is efficiency in commercial banking? How is efficiency measured? How can the holding company and merged system be reliably compared considering basic differences such as size, location, business mix, organizational form, legal factors, management, and markets. This study was not intended to, and cannot, resolve these questions.

[51] Bankshares and First and Merchants 1962–66 financial summaries are shown in Tables A-9 and A-10.

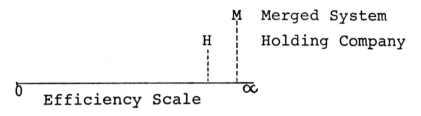

Fig. III-1. Efficiency scale. Assuming the merged system as a form of organization is more efficient than a holding company, because of closer integration of operations, it will be to the right of a holding company as measured by points *M* and *H*.

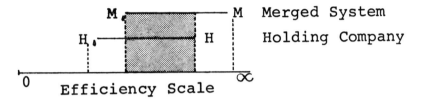

Fig. III-2. Efficiency scale. Assuming there is a range of efficiencies, depending on the objectives and policies of a particular management, integration of operations is likely to vary from bank to bank, and there could be any number of points on the scale where both forms are the same, as represented by the shaded area.

IV *Financial Considerations*

Literature

THE amount of credit extended to any single customer is limited by banking laws to 10 percent of the capital and surplus and undivided profits for individual national banks and at 15 percent of the capital and surplus for state-chartered banks in Virginia.[1] Expansion of individual banking systems inevitably increases the capital base necessary for the extension of larger lines of credit but does not necessarily improve the mobility of credit. On this latter point the critical question is whether the two forms of organization provide equal mobility of credit. Here the literature suggests, understandably, that in both the mobility is greater than in an independent bank. For example, in holding companies the combined lending power of all affiliated banks is available to any member institution to accommodate the financing requirements of large customers. And in merged systems, the credit line of any branch, regardless of size, is considered to be the same as that of the system as a whole. The full lending power of the home office is theoretically available at any branch office: "The branch system provides for mobility of funds and can shift excess reserves for lending through other outlets of the system. Thus, there are offices of some branch banks which have loan-deposit ratios of over 100 percent."[2] In an independent unit bank, credit mobility is limited because credit arrangements made through correspondents depend on the closeness of the correspondent relationship, which may vary so much as to restrict this form of lending.[3]

In a comparison of the two forms of expansion, the mobility of

[1] Bureau of Banking of the State Corporation Commission, *Laws of Virginia Relating to Banking and Finance* (Charlottesville, Va.: Michie Co., 1966), p. 27. The 15-percent limit for state-chartered banks in Virginia is specified in article 7, section 6.1–61.

[2] Bernard Shull and Paul M. Horvitz, "Branch Banking and the Structure of Competition," *Studies in Banking Competition and the Banking Structure* (Washington, D.C.: Comptroller of the Currency, 1966), p. 135.

[3] W. Ralph Lamb, *Group Banking: A Form of Banking Concentration and Control in the United States* (New Brunswick, N.J.: Rutgers University Press, 1962), p. 239.

funds seems to be potentially greater in merged systems because of certain legal and operating constraints on holding companies. Until 1966, section 6 of the Bank Holding Company Act of 1956 limited credit mobility by requiring loan participation within holding companies to be made "at the outset" of the loan transaction. On this point Robert J. Lawrence commented:

But Section 23a of the Federal Reserve Act was amended so that its restrictions on banking affiliates were also applied to the subsidiaries of bank holding companies. These restrictions state that a banking affiliate may not loan or otherwise extend credit to another affiliate or to the holding company if the total amount of loans or extension of credit to the other affiliate exceeds 10 percent of the lending affiliate's capital and surplus or if the total amount of loans or extensions of credit to all affiliates (including the holding company) exceeds 20 percent of the lending affiliate's capital and surplus. (Under the original act, loans from one banking subsidiary to another or to the holding company, that is, "cross-stream" and "up-stream" loans, were prohibited.) However, because the purchase of loan paper without recourse is not considered an extension of credit, it appears no significant restrictions now exist on the purchase of loan paper by one subsidiary from another or loan participation between subsidiaries.[4]

Yet, even with the elimination of the "outset restriction," holding companies had the problem of arranging loan participation among affiliates, separate banks which may not be wholly owned. This situation differs from that in branch systems, where any branch office may lend the legal maximum to any single customer. Consequently, the extension of large lines of credit beyond the loan limits of a single holding company unit may be less easy to arrange, in practice, than comparable loans in the branch system. However, a distinction needs to be drawn between what a branch may legally do and what it actually does in practice. Operating limits are normally placed on the lending authority of branch managers, which would necessitate a type of participation from the home office for any loan larger than that authorized.

One obvious difference between holding companies and merged organizations is that the mobility of funds in holding companies is related to the responsibility of the directors in affiliated banks, who have legal responsibilities irrespective of participation agreements or the lending policies of the holding company. Where affiliates are not 100 percent owned, the directors have a clear responsibility to all stockholders in the movement of funds, dividends, up-and-

---

[4] Robert J. Lawrence, *The Performance of Bank Holding Companies* (Washington, D.C.: Board of Governors of the Federal Reserve System, 1967), p. 10.

down-stream loans, rates on such loans, and other matters involving the profitability of the individual bank.

Numerous sources cite increased financial strength as a characteristic of both forms of expansion in comparison with the unit bank.[5] Typically, the expanded organizations have large capital bases and, with few exceptions, serve extensive marketing areas through their affiliates and branches. Large size and extensive marketing areas make it possible to have a great variety of loans in the portfolio and thus to spread the risk over a large operating base. Branch systems must limit their loan-to-asset ratio, but not at any one office.

Its overall ratio will depend on loan demand in many areas, not just one. Some offices may have loan ratios that would be too low to be profitable for a unit bank; others may have ratios too high to be safe for a unit bank. In aggregate, the ratio may be higher than the average of a group of unit banks similarly situated because funds are more efficiently transferred from office to office in a branch system, and because the risks of illiquidity associated with deposit withdrawals are spread over a larger base and thereby reduced.[6]

Another advantage of both forms is flexibility in acquiring capital. Today, both banks and holding companies may use equity and debt financing. This was not always the case.

The sale of debentures by commercial banks is a relatively recent development. Before 1933, banks relied upon common stock and retained earnings for capital funds. Indeed, neither national nor state bank legislation authorized the issuance of either preferred stock or debt securities.[7]

Until 1962, when new regulations were issued by the Comptroller of the Currency, debenture financing by banks in the United States is said to have been dominated by the adverse attitude of regulatory authorities at both the national and the state level.[8] The Comptroller's new regulation permitted national banks to issue convertible or nonconvertible capital debentures up to 100 percent of unimpaired paid-in capital stock plus 50 percent of unimpaired surplus funds. National banks were also permitted to issue preferred stock,

[5] Palmer T. Hogenson, *The Economies of Group Banking* (Washington, D.C.: Public Affairs Press, 1955), pp. 139, 142, 144; Lamb, p. 234; Lawrence, p. 6; Federal Reserve Bank of Richmond, "The New Look in Banking Structure," *Monthly Review*, July 1963, p. 3.

[6] Shull and Horvitz, p. 150.

[7] George W. McKinney, Jr., "New Sources of Bank Funds: Certificate of Deposit and Debt Securities," *Law and Contemporary Problems*, XXXII (Winter 1967), 85.

[8] *Ibid.*, pp. 86–87.

convertible or nonconvertible, without limitations as to capital and surplus. By June 1964 most state regulatory agencies had followed the lead of the Comptroller: "all but fourteen states had authorized the use of debentures, and only four prohibited the use of both preferred stock and debentures."[9]

In view of these developments in bank debt financing, the critical question is whether the two forms of bank expansion have the same flexibility in acquiring capital. The literature suggests that both forms enjoy flexibility as the result of increased size, because to a greater extent than formerly, their stocks are traded on regional and national exchanges and reported by security dealers.[10]

On the other hand, economists who have analyzed bank holding companies have consistently concluded that their subsidiaries have significant advantages over independent banks in acquiring capital.[11] One of the strongest arguments is that the parent usually has the capacity to supply affiliated banks with additional capital as required by their growing volume of business.[12] Also, according to one study, a billion-dollar holding company may sell its stock at rates often competitive with even the largest independent banks in the area, whereas a small group system apparently has little advantage, since affiliates usually raise their own capital. However, "a small bank which is the member of a very large group system finds it possible to secure added funds via the group at a substantial saving."[13] Moreover, Fischer finds that small banks are able to attract large amounts of equity funds from new investors as well as from their own shareholders. He concludes that no small bank is necessarily prevented from selling stock as a consequence of size alone. However, small banks infrequently raise equity capital because it usually must be offered at a discount from book value, and because the owners of closely held banks do not wish to lose control of the banks.[14]

Holding companies enjoy certain advantages in the acquisition of capital: they can raise capital at either the parent or affiliated bank level, or both, whereas merged systems can do so only at the

[9] *Ibid.*, p. 90.

[10] *Bank Stock Quarterly*, a publication of M. A. Shapiro and Company, Inc., underwriters, brokers, and dealers in bank stocks, reports on selected commercial banks and holding companies.

[11] Lawrence, p. 7. One reason is that the shares are usually traded in national or regional markets.

[12] Lamb, p. 148.

[13] Gerald C. Fischer, *Bank Holding Companies* (New York: Columbia University Press, 1961), pp. 124–25.

[14] *Ibid.*, p. 127.

bank level; holding companies have no restrictions on the use of debt, whereas merged systems have limitations on debentures, and notes maturing in less than one year must be counted as liabilities requiring reserves. These differences imply that holding companies have more flexibility in raising capital. However, no empirical evidence conclusively demonstrates that the result is some tangible economic benefit, such as a lower cost of capital or greater earnings per share from the use of leverage. Consequently, the flexibility advantage of the holding company may be less significant than it appears. Empirical studies of the cost of capital-to-capital structure relationship in merged systems and holding companies may be useful in clarifying this issue.

An advantage of both forms of expansion is that they may become large and strong enough to compete effectively with outside financial centers in supplying credit.

By building groups that have substantial amounts of banking funds concentrated in the hands of compact organizations, adequate banking resources will be available at all times which will not be subject to the influences foreign to the needs of these regions.[15]

Consequently, credit inflow is reduced, and a region's dependence on outside financial centers is lessened. In fact, this argument was cited as justification for liberalizing Virginia's banking legislation in 1962, in order to increase the size of individual banking organizations in the state.

RESEARCH FINDINGS

Credit and Funds Mobility

Mobility of funds was an advantage cited by both organizations studied. According to Bankshares, the holding company had this advantage not in relation to a merged system but to an individual bank in Virginia. On the other hand, First and Merchants suggested that a merged system might have greater potential than a holding company in this area.

First and Merchants' management thought that the merged form had greater potential for credit mobility because a branch in an area could have a loan-deposit ratio of 100 percent or even more since a branch was constrained only by the limits placed on the system as a whole.[16] Although a holding company competitor

[15] Hogenson, p. 144.   [19] Green, personal communication, 1968.

in the area could theoretically place the same amount of loans with the participation of affiliated banks, an officer of First and Merchants argued that participation among several banks did not work too well in practice.

Participation must go through the separate boards of directors of a holding company, and each may not react the same way. The extension of credit is personal judgment—it is not an exact science by any manner of means. While the holding company could say what will be done in a certain situation, the board of directors of an affiliate is still required by law to exercise independent judgment, or be subject to legal action.[17]

Bankshares' position was that holding companies, like merged systems, had the capability of pooling resources for loans among affiliates.[18] To facilitate the flow of funds throughout its system, Bankshares developed a loan-participation procedure by which large loans that needed to be shared throughout the system were cleared in advance. In the opinion of an officer of Bankshares, the use of rapid communication devices, central credit files, charge cards, and data-processing equipment would ultimately remove any advantage enjoyed by branch systems in the area of credit mobility.

As a practical matter, the question of mobility of funds is directly related to the responsibility of the directors in the organization. Because of this fact the holding company does not enjoy the same mobility of funds as the merged system, in which there is only one board of directors. In moving funds within a holding company, the directors of the individual affiliates have legal responsibilities and liabilities not mitigated in any sense by a standard participation agreement or lending policy. These legal restrictions particularly apply where the affiliates are less than 100 percent owned, for here the directors are required to protect the rights of minority stockholders in the same way they protect the rights of the holding company. As a consequence, directors of affiliates may have conflicting views on matters relating to fund mobility, a fact which, from a practical standpoint, could constrain movement of funds throughout a holding company system. For instance, under conditions of credit rationing, directors of affiliates might face the choice of satisfying the loan demand in their local service area or participating in loans of prime importance to the holding company. The matter of director responsibility would probably not generate a problem in funds mobility during,

[17] *Ibid.*
[18] Lewis B. Flinn, Jr., personal communication, 1968.

say, nine out of ten working days. Whenever it did come up, however, it would be most unwelcome to management.

Through 1966 there appears to have been no significant difference between the systems studied with respect to funds mobility. The data on Bankshares and First and Merchants in figure IV-1

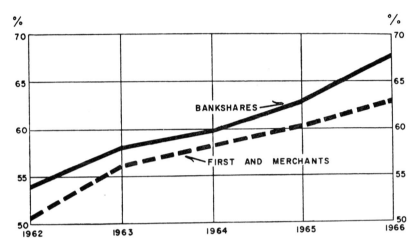

Fig. IV-1. Loan-to-deposit ratio, First and Merchants and Bankshares, 1962–1966. Data from 1967 *Annual Report* of United Virginia Bankshares (for 1963–66); secretary treasurer of United Virginia Bankshares (for 1962); *Annual Report* of First and Merchants National Bank (for 1962–66). 1962 data for Bankshares are on a *pro forma* basis for the original six members.

suggest that expansion of loans, measured as a percentage of deposits, was comparable, assuming equally able loan officers in each organization and equally good lending opportunities in each banking community.

Mobility of funds within a branch structure also depends on the types of locality that branches serve; in some localities deposits will exceed loan demand (wealthy urban communities); in some loan demand will exceed deposits (business communities); and in others loans and deposits will just about balance. Consequently it is difficult to generalize about comparative mobility of funds not only between holding companies and merged systems but also among individual holding companies and individual merged systems. A relevant question for bank management appears to be: Which type of organization uses the different types of locations for banks to best advantage? For instance, does one method of expansion do better in localities of high loan demand, where the customers are firms with multiplant or multioffice locations elsewhere in the state?

Raising and Using Capital

Both First and Merchants and Bankshares cited financial flexibility as an advantage of their respective forms of expansion. However, Bankshares' use of the term was broader than First and Merchants' in that it concerned both raising and allocating capital, and it was more consistent with the concept of financial flexibility in the literature. The managements of both Bankshares and First and Merchants quite possibly have equally valid points of view, depending on the respective definition of the term.

First and Merchants' management believed the merged system resulted in greater financial flexibility because one capital account was easier to control and manipulate than capital accounts in many independent units.[19] Also, it was the position of First and Merchants that a bank name was an advantage when selling equity or debt in the local area. This advantage was explained by an officer of First and Merchants as follows:

To buy First and Merchants National Bank stock there is acceptability of the equity and debt instruments at the local community and this would be much greater than it would be for a holding company that does not identify to any bank. Today there is a problem, so the bankers say, in the identification of a holding company with a bank in the community, i.e., people in the community tend to get mixed up. However, this does not apply to a sophisticated investor, but to the man in the street, it does.[20]

Bankshares' management preferred the holding company because it had more flexibility in the raising of capital.[21] Two reasons were given: (1) financing could be done either by affiliated banks or by the holding company (2) financing could be done in more ways and with more ease than in a merged system. Also, the use of leverage and the raising of capital at low cost were said to be important benefits:

The potential of the holding company is to maximize leverage, using debt financing to a greater extent than through a bank. After all, the examiners who examine banks are going to be more restrictive on how much debt they are going to allow a bank to issue. They would not have the same concern about a holding company since we do not have any depositors. It is a different thing if we go under. If we fail it has nothing

19 Green, personal communication, 1968.
20 *Ibid.*
21 Flinn, personal communication, 1968.

to do with the banks. We are just the stockholder. The stockholder can go broke, but the bank is still in operation. . . .

We could issue short-term debt at a rate we wanted and that the market would permit. If a bank tried to do the same thing there would probably be a limitation on the rate. If the debt instrument was construed as a deposit by the Federal Reserve Board then it would be subject to reserve requirements and to the rate limitations of Regulation Q. I don't think any holding company yet has maximized the possibilities. But every now and then you see where a holding company has improved leverage through the use of debt financing.[22]

The greater financial flexibility of the holding company, in comparison with the merged system, is illustrated by the case of State-Planters. The bank could not provide the owner of property needed for a new building with a tax-free transaction, because the bank could not issue stock, except under stock options, in a cash sale or in a merger. However, a holding company can obtain property on a tax-free basis by exchanging its stock for land.

In their importance to management, there appear to be some essential differences between the forms of expansion with respect to control of the capital account. The control seems more complicated in the holding company. In a merged system the transfer of capital funds is internal to one corporation, whereas in a holding company more than one corporation is involved. In the holding company problems may arise involving minority interest and the responsibilities of directors on such issues as dividend policy, rates on up-and-down-stream loans,[23] and allocation of costs to affiliates for services of the holding company. Furthermore, in the merged system there are one accounting system and one set of financial statements, whereas in the holding company each affiliate has its own statements and may have its own accounting system. Consequently, the operating results of the individual affiliates are generally a matter of public record for shareholders and investors, whereas in the merged system branch profitability is an internal matter. Together these differences suggest that management in the merged system probably has more direct control over the use of capital because the matter is internal to one corporation and one body of stockholders.

[22] *Ibid.*

[23] Section 23A of the amended Federal Reserve Act permits loans between affiliates—both bank affiliates and holding company subsidiaries—with the restrictions that the total amount loaned to one affiliate shall not exceed 10 percent of the lending affiliate's capital and surplus, and that the total amount to all affiliates shall not exceed 20 percent of the lending affiliate's capital and surplus.

The issue raised by First and Merchants concerning the value of a bank's name in selling its stock involves assumptions about the motivations of buyers of stock and suppliers of capital. Clearly, there are different kinds of buyers with different motivations and objectives in the capital markets. Consequently, most arguments as to whether unit banks, holding companies, or merged systems can raise capital most easily are meaningless in the sense that they omit considerations of the basic issue: Who, what, and where is the market for different kinds of securities? Each situation, in essence, depends on these considerations.

Any significant advantage of the holding company in flexibility of raising capital should result in some definitive economic benefit. This benefit might be a lower cost of capital or improved access to the capital markets, since these factors influence profitability and growth. Consequently, the critical question is whether the benefits of one form of expansion are significantly greater than those of the other.

Both forms of expansion may use equity and debt financing, but because there are fewer constraints on the use of debt financing in the holding company, it appears to have a greater potential for financial leverage. First, as suggested by Bankshares, the holding company may be able to handle more debt than a bank because the regulatory agencies are not concerned with protecting depositors at the holding company level. Use of short-term promissory notes by banks, authorized by the Comptroller of the Currency (Saxon) in 1963, was virtually terminated by the fact that the board of governors of the Federal Reserve System classified them as deposits. This ruling made short-term notes subject to the reserve and interest ceiling rate requirements of the Federal Reserve System.[24] Holding companies are under no such constraint.

Second, limitations on the use of capital debentures or notes specified for national banks by the Comptroller do not apply to holding companies.

The principal amount of capital debentures outstanding at any time, when added to all other outstanding indebtedness of the bank, except those forms of indebtedness exempt from the provisions of 12 U.S.C. 82, shall not exceed an amount equal to 100 percent of the bank's unimpaired paid-in capital stock plus 50 percent of the amount of its unimpaired surplus fund.[25]

[24] McKinney, p. 98.
[25] *Ibid.*, p. 90.

Moreover, the nonbanking nature of a holding company may result in a more liberal attitude on the part of its management toward the use of debt. This possibility is suggested by the comment of a Bankshares officer that the holding company could "go under" and the individual banks would not be affected, at least directly. These differences suggest that management in a holding company could justify the use of extensive debt in order to maximize leverage and under such conditions might reduce the long run cost of capital.[26]

On the other hand, a reduction in the cost of capital may be more a function of the size of an organization than of the type. One study reports that large holding companies are able to sell their stock at rates often competitive with the largest independent banks in an area.[27] This finding implies comparable capital costs for large organizations of both forms of expansion rather than an advantage to either. Furthermore, assuming all other factors affecting the cost of capital are comparable, the data in Table IV-1 suggest that there was no significant difference in Virginia between the three holding companies using debt and the two merged systems not using debt during the years 1965–66.[28] The holding companies, as of December 31, 1966, had debt-to-equity ratios ranging from a low of 24.9 to a high of 43 percent; debt was financed at rates ranging from 4¾ to 4⅞ percent.

However, to the extent that the three holding companies have been able to use debt financing at these rates in place of higher cost equity, and in view of the fact that interest on debt is a deductible expense, they may have gained some economic benefit not reflected in the admittedly rough approximation of cost of capital shown in Table IV-1.

The cost-of-capital issue narrows down to two possible conclusions: (1) that, because of its greater potential for leverage, which may result in a reduced long-run cost of capital, the holding

[26] This assumption is based on the traditional viewpoint in finance that a firm's cost of capital may be lowered by the use of a judicious amount of debt.

[27] Fischer, *Bank Holding Companies*, pp. 124–25. The study also reports that small holding companies apparently have little advantage in lowering capital costs since affiliates usually raise their own capital, but a small bank in a large system may get additional capital at considerable savings.

[28] Comparison of the average cost of capital indicates a t value of .37. With 2 degrees of freedom, a t value as large as 6.965 will occur by chance alone with a probability of .95 when the samples are from the same distribution. These data, therefore, do not support the hypothesis that the samples are from different distributions.

Table IV-1. Cost-of-capital: Three holding companies
and two merged systems in Virginia, 1965–66

	Holding companies	Merged systems
Year	Weighted cost of equity and debt (percent) *	Cost of equity (percent)
1965	6.2	6.3
1966	7.4	8.1
Average	6.8	7.2

SOURCES: Data from J. C. Wheat and Company, Richmond, Va., *Virginia Bank Stocks Annual Review*, 1965–66;
and the 1965–66 annual reports of First and Merchants National Bank, First Virginia Corporation, Virginia Commonwealth Corporation, Virginia National Bank, and
United Virginia Bankshares Incorporated.

* The cost of equity capital is approximated by the earn-
ings-price ratio; the cost of long-term debt is approximated
by the rate on outstanding debt.

company benefits more than the merged system; or (2) that there
is no significant difference as suggested by experience with the two
forms of expansion in Virginia. The first of these choices is thought
to be the better because the validity of the quantitative data supporting the no-difference hypothesis is severely limited by the small
sample, the short time span measured, and the admittedly rough
approximation of cost of capital. Consequently, clarification of the
economic consequences of this issue can come only from empirical
research after the banking industry as a whole adopts practices
that make more effective use of debt financing.

Economic Benefits to the Shareholders
of the Acquired Bank

Only Bankshares cited economic benefits for the shareholders of
the acquired bank as a significant consideration in selecting a form
of expansion. It was identified, however, as an advantage applicable
to both forms. Bankshares' management thought that the financial
terms of an acquisition were important, and in some cases decisive,
in a bank's decision to join their holding company.[29] Their policy
was to acquire banks on a book value basis adjusted to reflect current value of assets. The economic benefit to the stockholders re-

[29] Flinn, personal communication, 1968.

sulted from the fact that their stock, like that of many small banks in Virginia, generally sold at or below book value. On the other hand, Bankshares stock generally sold above book value—at times by as much as 100 percent. An officer of Bankshares illustrated this point as follows:

Assume you are a large holding company or a large bank and your stock is selling at a substantial price above book. You can afford to offer somebody book for book and at the same time give him, say, 100 percent appreciation on what he can get for his stock on the market. . . . It is hard to gauge the influence that this has, but it is important. It may be the real clincher. We also talk to management about local autonomy, tell them how we operate, etc. We tell them the two or three requirements that you have to hammer on: (1) that their board is responsible for running the show, (2) that Bankshares as a stockholder is basically a service organization, (3) that we are interested in doing bigger and grander things and most importantly to earn some money for our stockholders. But, who knows really how much impact philosophy has versus the dollar?[30]

Premiums for banks in Virginia interested in joining a system are less likely in the future because speculative interest in merger candidates has increased the value of the stock of banks with acquisition potential.

Table IV-2. Bankshares' and First and Merchants' stock prices in relation to book value, 1962–66

Year	Bankshares	First and Merchants
	(percentage of book value)	
1962		167
1963	190	180
1964	200	210
1965	202	183
1966	183	163

SOURCE: Data from J. C. Wheat and Company, Richmond, Va., *Virginia Bank Stocks Annual Review*, 1962–66.

The literature clearly supports the position that affiliation with a holding company can result in economic benefit to the acquired bank's shareholders. "Opportunity to gain a profitable premium through exchange of stock with a group" is among the three most

30 *Ibid.*

frequently cited reasons for joining a holding company.[31] However, as pointed out by Bankshares, this benefit is not limited to holding company affiliation. Direct merger also provides a premium to the shareholders of the acquired bank when the acquisition is made on a book-to-book basis and when the acquired bank's stock is selling at or below book value. In both cases the liquidity of the shares of big banking organizations is an important attraction. Premiums received are more commonly attributed to the better marketability of shares of big organizations than to almost any other factor.

Table IV-2 illustrates Bankshares' point that premiums over book value were common to both forms of expansion during the years 1962–66.

Diversification of Risk

Only First and Merchants cited diversification of risk as a significant consideration in the selection of a form of expansion. They preferred the merged form because it provided for greater diversification in the loan portfolio and investment account.[32]

The literature generally holds that large banking organizations of all types—unit banks, holding companies, and merged systems—are better able than small banks to diversify risk in their loan and investment portfolios. The large organizations typically serve markets of greater size, and when these areas have different economic characteristics, diversification can work to reduce the risk in the loan portfolio. Similarly, large banking organizations have more funds and can gain greater diversity in their investment portfolios, a fact that, theoretically at least, minimizes the impact of any one loss.

[31] Gerald C. Fischer, *American Banking Structure* (New York: Columbia University Press, 1968), p. 98. The most frequently cited reason for affiliation is the "desire of major stockholders for more liquid holdings."
[32] Green, personal communication, 1968.

V *Marketing Considerations*

LITERATURE

MARKETING characteristics of holding companies and merged systems are broadly discussed in the literature in terms of the quantity and quality of banking services. With few exceptions, big banks, whatever their form, offer a larger array of services and serve different markets and customers than small banks. What type of organization is best in this market of big organizations?

The literature argues that large banking organizations are generally more efficient than their smaller competitors and typically can offer more services at a lower unit cost to their customers. The most commonly cited marketing characteristics of the large banking organization are uniform banking facilities and services, increased and possibly improved (or less costly) banking services, stimulation of competition, and marketing identity.

Holding companies and merged systems both offer uniform banking facilities and services in that each affiliate or branch has access to the same array. Thus, any disparity between services available to metropolitan and to rural communities tends to be eliminated. One author argues that in holding companies, "country banks are able to receive the benefit of specialists in banking who can be maintained only by the large metropolitan banks. In this way every bank customer is assured the use of all services promptly and with little additional charge."[1] While nonaffiliated country banks theoretically can and do obtain similar services through their correspondent relationships, these relationships do not often provide the same degree of uniform "regional banking" that results from large merged systems and holding companies.

It is alleged in the literature that the banking needs of the region or community are best served by holding companies and merged systems because large lines of credit are available, along with extensive banking services. By having a large line of credit, these systems can best serve industry, which generally expands

---

[1] Palmer T. Hogenson, *The Economies of Group Banking* (Washington, D.C.: Public Affairs Press, 1955), p. 139.

more rapidly than banking.[2] Whereas small banks find it difficult to serve the relatively few customers who benefit from large lines of credit, the large systems can serve these typically important customers in broad regional or national markets and provide the specialized services they need. A resulting benefit is greater diversification of risk in the larger, more widespread banking organizations because they can commit greater proportions of potential bank credit to individual communities.[3] Moreover, the centralized research and service activities of both forms of expansion frequently benefit bank customers with broadened services at the local level.

Small unit banks are limited in the quality and selection of financial services they can offer the public whereas even the smallest group affiliate can make a great variety of specialized financial services readily available to bank customers.[4]

Because of the ability to centralize some functions, and because it is unnecessary to erect expensive buildings for each office, a branch system can provide full banking services in areas which could not support even a small unit bank offering limited services.[5]

Trust accounts and other areas of specialization are the most commonly cited examples of the extension of banking services. In such areas small unit banks are rarely able to employ competent specialists profitably. On the other hand, the large holding companies or branch systems ordinarily specialize in such areas as agriculture, industrial loans, and real estate. This advantage of system banking, however, obviously does not apply across the board to all customers and all markets. Certainly, there is no requirement for all banks to supply every service, if for no other reason than that some markets may not profitably support a full-service banking operation.

As previously pointed out, both forms of expansion generally benefit from economies of scale, centralization, and specialization. Because of this fact it is suggested that they bring more efficient and less costly banking services to the public. One study suggests that communities have better banking services following the entry

[2] W. Ralph Lamb, *Group Banking: A Form of Banking Concentration and Control in the United States* (New Brunswick, N.J.: Rutgers University Press, 1962), p. 235.

[3] Federal Reserve Bank of Richmond, "The New Look in Banking Structure," *Monthly Review,* July 1963, p. 3.

[4] Lamb, p. 235–36.

[5] Federal Reserve Bank of Richmond, "The New Look in Banking Structure," p. 3.

of holding companies. Loan-to-deposit ratios are higher, probably indicating better loan service, and the general level of interest rates does not increase.[6] Another study notes certain characteristics in the performance of affiliates in local market areas: increased supply of bank loans, increased accommodation of the credit needs of state and local government, higher customer service charges, not significantly higher time-deposit interest rates, no significant change in interest rates on loans, and no change in operating efficiency when measured in terms of expenses-to-revenues ratio.[7] With respect to merged systems, another study points to certain differences in the performance characteristics of unit banks and branch banks. In general, after mergers the community benefits from expansion in the number of services offered by the branch banks and in lower costs for some service functions: "Interest on time deposits rose, loan rates generally fell, and loan terms and lending authority were generally extended at the acquired bank. Service charges on checking accounts were generally increased at the acquired bank."[8]

While the literature and empirical evidence suggest that the public benefits from greater services and possibly lower costs from the two forms of expansion, the findings are not considered absolute. A summary of banking research states that branch banking and performance relationships may be influenced by factors other than the prevalent form of banking organization.

In particular, branch and unit banking follow fairly definite geographic patterns in the United States, suggesting that regional differences in demand or in the character of state banking regulations could have pronounced effects on bank performance that may not properly be attributed to organizational characteristics.[9]

Seven studies agree only that branch banks usually have higher net earnings relative to capital and higher loan-to-asset ratios than unit banks in the same state.[10] Consequently, findings in the area of efficiency and profitability of unit banking as opposed to system

[6] Gerald C. Fischer, *Bank Holding Companies* (New York: Columbia University Press, 1961), pp. 130–34.

[7] Robert J. Lawrence, *The Performance of Bank Holding Companies* (Washington, D.C.: Board of Governors of the Federal Reserve System, 1967), p. 24.

[8] Bernard Shull and Paul M. Horvitz, "Branch Banking and the Structure of Competition," *Studies in Banking Competition and the Banking Structure* (Washington, D.C.: Comptroller of the Currency, 1966), pp. 176–77.

[9] Federal Reserve Bank of Chicago, "Competition in Banking: What is Known? What Is the Evidence?" *Business Conditions*, February 1967, pp. 11–12.

[10] *Ibid.*, p. 12.

banking are at best only suggestive—substantial quantitative evidence is lacking.

That expansion by either method stimulates competition among banking institutions is not universally held in the literature. Some economists, bankers, and public officials believe that branch banking is "an essentially procompetitive form of banking that facilitates the penetration of additional banking markets and brings to bear the force of potential competition on even the smallest and most isolated banking markets."[11] A study comparing Vermont statewide branching with New Hampshire unit banking claims that statewide branching "also seems to have instigated slightly more competition, although this might be caused by other factors."[12] And the same benefits are attributed to holding company operations: "The public is the beneficiary of these activities, especially as they stimulate unit bankers in the area to improve banking services in order to maintain their positions in the market."[13]

On the other hand, the opponents of branching, whether accomplished through holding companies or by direct mergers, argue that it is monopolistic and tends to restrict competition. This controversy, of course, is still unresolved. It involves many political and economic considerations in the continuing public debate over unit versus multiple-unit banking. The examination of this issue is not within the scope of this study.

The holding company has greater flexibility in selecting its marketing identity than does the merged system. A bank that has served a community for many years—one with an outstanding reputation—may continue to use its local name after affiliation with a holding company. On the other hand, where the acquiring holding company's name (for example, Marine Midland Banks, Incorporated, Buffalo, New York) may be better for marketing identification, an affiliate may take on the identity of its parent. By way of contrast, in expansion by direct merger the acquired bank takes the name of the acquiring bank, thereby losing the benefit of local identity in markets where it may be important.

---

[11] Federal Reserve Bank of Chicago, "Competition in Banking: The Issues," *Business Conditions,* January 1967, p. 15.

[12] Federal Reserve Bank of Boston, "What Price Branching? Banking in Vermont and New Hampshire," *Business Review,* August 1964, p. 2.

[13] Lamb, p. 238.

RESEARCH FINDINGS

Larger Lines of Credit

First and Merchants argued that expansion by direct merger resulted in an increased line of credit for any one customer as the
result of increased capital.[14] Bankshares also saw this as an advantage to expansion by the holding company route.

First and Merchants in 1962 could lend one customer approximately $1.5 million; nine Virginia banks were required to par-
ticipate to lend $5 million. However, after expansion of its capital
as the result of mergers, First and Merchants could lend approximately $3.5 million in 1966, and only a few large Virginia banks
were needed to lend $5 million. In the absence of the law per-
mitting mergers, the banks' capital structure could be increased
only through retained earnings or the sale of additional stock. An
officer of First and Merchants expressed the opinion that capital
funds would have been greatly reduced had not mergers taken
place. He also stated First and Merchants had still not reached the
desired size when measured by either capital or deposits.

Large lines of credit are important in ways not discussed by
First and Merchants, and are common to both forms of expansion
as a function of increased size of the organization, independent of
the corporate form.

Large lines of credit are needed in only a small proportion of a
bank's business, involving, say, 1 to 5 percent of the borrowers in
any given market area. However, these few borrowers have considerable significance with regard to the total volume of loans.
Furthermore, a large line of credit is an important defensive shield
in keeping other large banks from acquiring business in the "home
area" banking community. And, at the same time, it provides a
bank with an opportunity to operate in an expanded market. These
considerations were clearly recognized by bankers in Virginia in
justifying the need for larger banking units in 1961 and were
important in bringing about liberalized legislation on branching
in 1962.

Virginia is surrounded by banks in North Carolina, Maryland, and the
District of Columbia with greater lending ability than any of the Virginia banks.

Consequently, the financing for big commercial and industrial projects

[14] John Green, personal communication, 1968.

in Virginia is being supplied by out-of-state banks with increasing frequency. These big loans are profitable business for the banks and they create deposits. . . .

Beyond doubt, Virginia bankers say, this state is losing banking business to North Carolina. A recent example was the H. K. Porter Co., whose $2,650,000 electrical transformer plant at Lynchburg was financed by a North Carolina bank and whose Disston Saw Division in Danville, which cost $1,500,000 to $2,000,000, was also financed in North Carolina.

No single Virginia bank could have made those loans, but either of two banks in North Carolina could.

The implications found in North Carolina financing of Virginia commerce and industry are important. If the borrower establishes banking connections in North Carolina, it perhaps becomes plausible for him to build his next plant or expansion in North Carolina instead of Virginia.[15]

An enlarged line of credit is primarily a function of the increase in organization size, regardless of the corporate form. This position is consistent with the literature and the experiences of the organizations studied. Figure V-1 compares the capital of First and Mer-

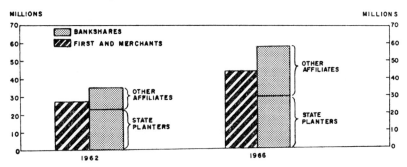

Fig. V-1. Capital of First and Merchants, Bankshares, and State-Planters for the years 1962 and 1966. Data from 1967 *Annual Report* of United Virginia Bankshares (for 1963–66); secretary treasurer of United Virginia Bankshares (for 1962); *Annual Report* of First and Merchants National Bank (for 1962–66). 1962 data for Bankshares are on a *pro forma* basis for the original six members.

chants with that of Bankshares for the years 1962–66; at the same time it compares First and Merchants with State-Planters, the largest single bank in Bankshares.

If the lending limit of State-Planters as a single bank is the measure of Bankshares' credit line, First and Merchants was larger in 1962 and 1966. However, if First and Merchants is compared with Bankshares on a system basis, Bankshares had the larger

15 Richmond *Times-Dispatch*, July 2, 1961.

credit line. In this case a system-to-system comparison is the more meaningful representation of the lending power of the two forms of expansion:

In effect, the combined capital accounts of the banks within a group system permit any local member institution to accommodate the financing requirements of the larger customers. While similar arrangements exist between independent unit banks through correspondents, the closeness of these relationships varies so much as to limit the application of this form of lending. In those group systems whose banking operations are supplemented by branch offices the flow of funds between areas is promoted even further by virtue of the branch form of organization.[16]

Marketing Identity

Both managements considered the question of marketing identity, each alleging certain advantages and disadvantages of a system image versus a local image.

First and Merchants recognized that one disadvantage of expansion by merger was that the acquired bank lost its name since it became an office of the acquiring bank. Several points concerning the importance of the merged bank's name were made to explain this situation to management, stockholders, and customers.[17] In some cases, management of the bank to be merged placed a great deal of emphasis on its local identity. A First and Merchants officer stated: "It is surprising how important an existing bank's name can be to the bank's management. In many instances bank management just does not want the name to disappear, and under the holding company route the name can be continued."[18]

In other cases, First and Merchants' management believed that the surviving bank's name was more important to the acquired bank's stockholders. If a bank were merged, the local stockholders would receive First and Merchants stock, that is, shares in a local bank as opposed to shares in a holding company, which might be located in some other area. Here management believed the stockholder's tie to a local bank was stronger and provided just as much local identity in a merged system as did the retention of the name for a bank joining a holding company.

First and Merchants' management found that customer acceptance of its name was excellent in the local community. A survey made in the Tidewater area indicated that 80 percent of the

[16] Lamb, p. 239.
[17] C. Coleman McGehee, personal communication, 1968.
[18] *Ibid.*

old depositors, who had for years been doing business with the acquired bank, associated with First and Merchants twenty-four months after merger.

Bankshares' position was that marketing identity worked both for and against the holding company.[19] A Bankshares officer said that it was an advantage in local markets where the banking relationship tended to be highly personal and where the customer had a long-standing banking association. On the other hand, the single corporate image of a merged system—or a holding company using a standard identification, such as Marine Midland—tended to be a more important marketing characteristic in urban areas where the customer was attracted to a large branch system by the uniformity of services. Here, an account was good in any branch in the market area, whereas in a holding company each member was a separate bank. However, Bankshares' management believed that disadvantages stemming from the separate identity of holding company affiliates could be offset to a degree by having wire service verification, uniform name, and a corporate symbol. Bankshares took both of these steps as did the First Virginia Bankshares Corporation.[20]

[19] Lewis B. Flinn, Jr., personal communication, 1968.

[20] Bankshares started operations without system identification at the local level but in 1968 announced that affiliates would assume a common identification in early 1969. A Bankshares press release stated:

"J. Harvie Wilkinson, Jr., President of the United Virginia Bankshares Incorporated, announced today that after lengthy study and consultation with the firm of Lippincott & Margulies in New York City as well as consumer representatives in several of the United Virginia Bankshares cities that all member banks of United Virginia Bankshares will adopt a program of common identification in early 1969. In commenting on this move before a conference of bank directors from each of the member banks, Mr. Wilkinson referred to the move as a forward step dictated by two geo-economic factors. He referred to the increasing mobility of our population in which 20% of our people change locations each year and in Virginia 90% of those changing locations make their changes to other locations in the state. Wilkinson also called attention to the economic necessity of taking full advantage of overlapping communications and promotional media, a practice which can be substantially augmented by a uniform identification.

"The first step in this program was naming the corporation's 'Edge Act' subsidiary United Virginia Bank International, followed by giving the name *United* Virginia BankAmericard to the credit care offered by UVB members. Subsequent plans call for a newly designed common logo and for each member bank to be known as 'United Virginia Bank' in its respective community and branch trading areas. In order to achieve the continuing local identification presently considered such a valuable part of the holding company concept, an identifying separatism will be achieved by the addition of a localizing suffix.

In the literature strong support is given holding companies on the issue of the local identity of an affiliate. However, from a marketing point of view, it seems impossible to generalize about the value of a bank's name. It varies with the individual circumstances. The value of a local bank name versus a system name depends on such considerations as the areas and the types of customers being served. As Bankshares argued, in small communities or rural areas where population turnover is low and business and banking associations are of a long-standing and personal nature, the name of the local bank may be best for customer relations. On the other hand, a system name may be a valuable marketing asset in large urban communities or metropolitan centers, where population mobility is high, and banking services are more likely to be chosen on the basis of convenience and uniformity. Management may also weigh the importance of identity in terms of the customer's banking alternatives. For example, local identity is of little consequence if there is no other bank in the community. In such a situation, the bank's name may be dropped as the result of a merger without fear of losing customers.

From the viewpoint of the merged system, First and Merchants' position that merger provides local identity for a bank's shareholders is valid. Their stock carries the name of their bank, whereas a holding company shareholder does not hold stock in the name of any bank, unless a uniform holding company identification like Marine Midland's is employed. However, this factor does not seem so significant as that of a bank's name with regard to different markets and customers. Any benefit is limited by the relatively

---

Plans when successfully concluded will result in member banks in United Virginia Bankshares operating under new names as follows: In Richmond—United Virginia Bank/State Planters; in Norfolk—United Virginia Bank/Seaboard National. . . .

"Concluding his announcement of the identification program Wilkinson said, 'All of our members eagerly look forward to the execution of this new program. While in many instances our members have achieved success over a period of more than one hundred years with their previous old and respected names, our changing times demand changing images and we believe that nowhere is the demand for change today more noticeable and urgent than in the banking business.' "

A combination of local and system identification was adopted for the first time in Virginia in 1968 by the First Virginia Bankshares Corporation when it renamed the Cambria Bank of Christiansburg the First Virginia Bank of the Southwest. According to the president of First Virginia Bankshares, the other banks would be renamed as local conditions, such as expansion and mergers, dictated.

small number of shareholders as compared with total customers— First and Merchants had approximately 5,300 shareholders in 1966.

Services

Both First and Merchants and Bankshares cited the advantages of new and expanded services. First and Merchants suggested that a merged system might have greater potential in this area, whereas Bankshares cited expanded services as an advantage of both forms, as contrasted with the relatively small unit bank in Virginia.

First and Merchants preferred expansion by direct merger because greater community services were thought to be provided through this form of expansion.[21] All of the services and facilities of a merged system were available at the local level; that is, each branch office could perform any and all services just as if it were the main office.

This is something that definitely cannot be done to the same degree in a holding company organization. Direct contact with the specialist in the bank of your choice, as in a merged organization, appears to be a solution which would give the customer more confidence than in the holding company where the specialized services may be performed by a bank of another name, or the holding company.[22]

First and Merchants' management also argued that expansion by direct merger developed larger individual banking units, which were then able to offer larger lines of credit and a wider range of services: "Industry is more naturally drawn to the larger financial organizations which can better serve some of their needs."[23]

On the other hand, Bankshares' position was that both forms provided a greater range, depth, and quality of banking services to Virginia citizens than a typical unit bank.

A direct comparison, however, of holding companies and merged systems is difficult. This would depend on the service objectives of management and the needs of each market area. For example, First Virginia, operating primarily in Northern Virginia, emphasizes consumer business. Therefore, their service structure would be quite different from, say, First and Merchants, operating largely in the Central and Tidewater Virginia areas, which caters, in a fairly balanced manner, to both consumer and industrial accounts.[24]

According to Bankshares, service benefits stemmed from the ability of the holding company to employ specialists in such areas as

[21] Green, personal communication, 1968.   [22] *Ibid.*   [23] *Ibid.*
[24] Flinn, personal communication, 1968.

trusts, industrial accounts, and data processing. Services of Bankshares in the 1962–66 period were expanded in the municipal bond department, professional services program, college tuition loan program, computerized payroll service program, one-check payroll program, marketing department, and planned operations of credit card program.

The literature clearly holds that both forms of expansion provide greater range, depth, and quality of banking services as a benefit of increased size, irrespective of the form of corporate organization. The issue is whether one form does it more effectively.

Both organizations added new and expanded banking services to the growing number of communities they served. This action suggests that the literature and Bankshares' positions draw the more meaningful contrast, that is, between a small unit bank— which does not have and cannot afford specialized kowledge and competence in its own personnel and must rely on its correspondent banks for providing these services—and both forms of expansion, which can and do provide more and better services at the local level.

Furthermore, Bankshares certainly has a valid point regarding the difficulty of drawing a direct comparison between the services of large banking organizations. Management's marketing objectives and the areas and customers served are factors that influence service at the local level. Consequently, direct comparisons between the two forms are meaningless unless these circumstances are considered on an individual basis.

Marketing Strategy

First and Merchants and Bankshares each planned and implemented an expansion strategy aimed at the growth areas in Virginia. In the following section this strategy is examined in light of the results of their expansion programs during the years 1962–66.

First and Merchants' expansion by direct merger was planned on a statewide basis.[25] It was primarily directed at urban and industrial areas with above-average growth potential. Expansion was based on management's concept that growth in metropolitan areas was more assured than in rural areas. For this reason Northern Virginia, Tidewater urban areas, Roanoke, and Lynchburg were considered. Winchester, Harrisonburg, Staunton,

[25] Green, personal communication, 1968.

Waynesboro, Bristol, Martinsville, and Danville were also attractive because they had relatively assured industrial growth potential.

An officer of First and Merchants said that merger partners were considered from the standpoint of future development in their areas.

More opportunities to merge were turned down than have actually merged —about three to one. With some of the people that we have known for many, many years, the hardest decision to make was to say no, if according to our analysis, the areas that they represented did not have the required growth potential. Banks like these generally wanted: (1) to share in the future growth and earnings of the First and Merchants system, (2) to solve a management succession problem, or (3) to obtain more marketability for stockholders shares from the merger.[26]

First and Merchants' expansion strategy was highly selective. Management believed selectivity was sound even though other bankers contended it was foolish to turn down any merger because the state of Virginia was going to grow.

Bankshares' strategy also was to expand in growth areas and to become a statewide banking system.[27] Growth areas were defined as those above the average in population growth and industrial expansion. The urban corridor south from Washington to Richmond and east through Williamsburg to Newport News and Norfolk met this definition. Cities outside the corridor, such as Lynchburg, were seen as key locations for a statewide system. On this point, a Bankshares officer said:

Bankshares was interested in going into other cities that were not in the corridor in order to become statewide. Yet, we were not interested in picking small country banks, because they do not have growth potential in our opinion, and serve only a very limited area.[28]

The same officer observed that one major system in Virginia was employing a contrasting strategy in that it merged banks throughout the state in rural communities.

I don't know what they see in these areas. We have heard them say that they can take a bank and operate it so that it is going to earn so much on total assets. But, we feel we can do the same thing, but we are interested in growth rather than just keeping a small branch that is never going to amount to anything.[29]

The expansion of both First and Merchants and Bankshares seems to have been generally consistent with their marketing

26 *Ibid.*   27 Flinn, personal communication, 1968.   28 *Ibid.*   29 *Ibid.*

strategy. First and Merchants completed seven mergers during the 1962–66 period (Table A-11, Appendix A). These mergers gave the bank thirty-three new banking offices and provided entry into twelve new marketing areas.

Bankshares completed seven acquisitions during the period 1964–67 (Table A-8, Appendix A). In addition to the six forming members of the holding company, these acquisitions gave Bankshares thirty-five new offices in ten new marketing areas.

With few exceptions, the acquisitions of both organizations were growth oriented in keeping with their strategies. Five metropolitan areas were involved in their expansion programs, each having a population growth, over the period 1962–66, exceeding the 9.1 percent rate for the rest of the state. The growth rate of Washington, D.C.—Virginia part—was 32.5 percent; Richmond, 15.2; Norfolk-Portsmouth, 14.5; Lynchburg, 10.9.[30]

Seemingly the growth-area expansion strategy does not consider certain other growth and profit opportunities. First, if strictly followed, it excludes banks in low-growth areas that have a relatively high return on capital or that have a very low loan-to-deposit ratio and therefore surplus funds for immediate use in high-growth or high-return areas. Such combinations seem to offer interesting profit oportunities to an expanding system, which might make a merger attractive in a low-growth area. Also, screening acquisitions by area-growth potential eliminates the profit opportunities from management-induced growth, for example, where better management might improve profitability or the market share.

Competition in the areas served by First and Merchants, Bankshares, and other expanding systems appears to have increased. No statewide banking system served the Waynesboro-Staunton-Augusta County regional population center in 1961. Furthermore, the largest of the eight banks serving this area in 1961 had deposits of $15 million.[31] By the end of 1966, as Table A-4, Appendix A shows, this area was served by branches and affiliates of three banking systems, with system deposits ranging from $301 to $536 million, and by three smaller banks, with deposits ranging from $5.8 to $19 million.[32]

---

[30] Bureau of Population and Economic Research, *Estimates of the Population of Counties and Cities of Virginia as of July 1, 1966* (Charlottesville, Va.: Graduate School of Business Administration, University of Virginia, 1966), p. 8.

[31] Bureau of Population and Economic Research, "Virginia Banking Survey for Years of 1947, 1961 through 1966," unpublished statistics (Charlottesville, Va.: Graduate School of Business Administration, University of Virginia, 1966).

[32] *Ibid.*

The nature of banking competition in many of the areas served by the statewide systems has also changed. For example, First National of Waynesboro, by its 1964 merger with First and Merchants, was transformed from a bank with $11 million in deposits into a branch of a bank with over $250 million in deposits. By this conversion, the full resources and wide range of services of a large statewide institution—more than four times the combined size of all of the competing banks in the area just the year before—became available in the Waynesboro service area. Also, when more than one statewide system serves an area, a new type of competition exists—system-to-system competition—between large full-service banking organizations.

While it is sometimes argued that increased concentration by merger and holding company acquisitions lessens rather than increases competition, this does not appear to be true in Virginia. For example, Table A-4, Appendix A, shows that all of the metropolitan areas except Roanoke are served by three or more systems. Additionally, while the concentration of deposits in large banks in Virginia has increased since 1962, Virginia was not among the seventeen states that had a concentration ratio over 50 percent in 1965.[33]

Growth-area expansion strategy, however, may have an adverse impact on rural areas. Any service and cost benefits that statewide systems bring to the banking public tend to be limited to the urban markets. The implication is that neither organization cares about becoming statewide in a geographic sense. Consequently, this type of expansion strategy takes on the character of skimming off the cream. It tends to maximize growth opportunities for management, but it does not necessarily serve all segments of the public equally well. However, since banking facilities are a scarce resource, equal coverage cannot be given to all areas. Therefore, it may be that a skim-the-cream strategy actually serves the public interest, since too extensive expansion might waste resources.

Those who urge more extensive branching do so on the ground that large systems would open offices in places now served only by small banks and so not as fully serviced as places served by larger banks or their branches. On this, *our data indicate that banking services definitely increase with bank size.* It follows that services would rise if large banks opened offices in places now served only by small banks. However, this would not necessarily be in the public interest. Inspection of the particular cases

[33] Gerald C. Fischer, *American Banking Structure* (New York: Columbia University Press, 1968), pp. 334–35.

where small banks are less apt to provide the service than large ones
suggests that usually it is because there is little demand for this service
by the customers of the smaller banks. Thus, more extensive branching
conceivably at least could result in the rendering of excessive services, i.e.,
a misallocation or waste of resources. For the principal implication of
our data is that small banks as well as larger banks, regardless of size and
location, play a useful role in our society. They service neighborhoods.
It would be wasteful for them to provide many services normally offered
by other classes of banks. There is no neighborhood demand for the
services in question. As a corollary and most importantly, our data indicate that, in general, banking services are provided where a demand for
them exists.[34]

An economic planner, in allocating this scarce resource, would
likely assign facilities to areas where they would most quickly
produce the most significant results—in this case, in Virginia's
fast-growing industrial and urban areas served by First and Merchants and Bankshares.

A negative aspect of the growth-area strategy of both organizations is that it appears inconsistent with the argument that merger
and holding company affiliation provide a solution to the problem
of management succession in small banks. Clearly, the small low-
growth rural banks most likely to have succession problems are
excluded from the merger universe.

Nonmetropolitan banks, however, have not been left out of the
merger and holding company movement in Virginia. They account
for nearly 50 percent of the mergers in the 1962–66 period. Also,
other systems, such as Virginia National Bank, have a strategy of
acquiring banks in rural areas.

Other Elements of First and Merchants' Expansion Strategy

Both managements cited other elements of strategy important to
their acquisition plans. A strategy empoyed by First and Merchants was to avoid dilution of book value and earnings in
mergers while giving the merging bank's shareholders fair value for
their holdings.[35] Also, an officer of First and Merchants predicted
either a slowdown in their acquisitions or a modification of their
selective strategy because of the concern of regulatory agencies
over the size and extent of mergers and holding company acquisi-

---

[34] U.S. Congress, House, Committee on Banking and Currency, *A Study of
Selected Banking Services by Bank Size, Structure, and Location,* 82d Cong.,
2d sess. (Washington, D.C.: Government Printing Office, 1952) , p. 19.

[35] Green, personal communication, 1968.

tions and competition for the good banking locations.[36] The implication was that First and Merchants' management recognized these influences and saw the future need for a flexible strategy.

Clearly, First and Merchants' strategy to avoid dilution of book value and earnings per share is intended to benefit the stockholders as well as management. However, on two occasions since 1962, management has reported to stockholders a decrease in earnings as the result of merger activities: the 1963 and 1965 annual reports to stockholders attributed dilution of earnings per share to the issuances of additional shares of stock in mergers. This experience seems consistent with the finding of one study of mergers in Virginia that stockholders of banks expanding by merger do not get the same growth in earnings per share as stockholders of banks not merging.

Stockholder interests do not appear to be furthered by the bank mergers that have occurred in New York and Virginia. In fact, earnings per share in Virginia is significantly negatively associated with merger activity, perhaps indicating that there may well be conflict of interest between managers and stockholders, at least in the short run.[37]

But, as found in this study, lower earnings per share may be explained in part by start-up costs in a merged organization and the added costs of new and expanded services.[38] Consequently, the long run effect of expansion may be to increase growth in earnings per share relative to banks not expanding by merger.

The desire of First and Merchants to maintain a flexible strategy reflects appreciation by management that important external forces influence the merger picture in Virginia. Regulatory authorities through denials and policy statements influence the supply of candidates by giving bankers an idea of what size and type of mergers may be approved. Shortly after the 1962 legislation, the merger of the Colonial-American National Bank and First National Exchange Bank, both of Roanoke, was denied on the grounds that the former bank should be preserved as the nucleus of further statewide expansion. This action provides evidence that the merger of two relatively large banks in the same market area in Virginia probably would not be approved.

[36] *Ibid.*

[37] Kalman J. Cohen and Samuel Richardson Reid, "Effects of Regulations, Branching, and Mergers on Banking Structures and Performance," *Southern Economic Journal*, XXIV (October 1967), pp. 240–41.

[38] Green, personal communication, 1968.

Other Elements of Bankshares' Expansion Strategy

An important element of Bankshares' strategy was that it wanted to acquire a leading bank in a community, one with deposits over $10 million, if possible.[39] First, Bankshares wanted strong well-run banks in key locations. A Bankshares officer explained: "At the outset we were particularly interested in getting a leading bank in a community—one with a good reputation, good management, and one which was well established. We wanted to create a strong group."[40]

Although Bankshares was interested in acquiring one of the largest banks in an area, management believed that the Federal Reserve was less likely to approve such combinations. However, Bankshares did get the largest bank in Northern Virginia (First and Citizens of Alexandria—$61.8 million in deposits), and second largest in Richmond (State-Planters—$220.3 million), in Newport News (Citizens and Marine Jefferson—$18.9 million), and in Lynchburg (First National Trust and Savings—$33.6 million).

A second reason for acquiring a leading bank was that its staff could operate on their own without day-to-day supervision. Given a choice, Bankshares preferred banks with deposits over $25 million. An officer explained this policy as follows:

You have more problems with banks under $10 million and have to spend more time working with them. We have a small staff, whereas Virginia Commonwealth and First Virginia operate, by and large, with a large holding company staff. A larger staff allows them to acquire more smaller banks. . . .

In such cases these banks (banks over $10 million) run themselves except for some of the sophisticated services that the holding company can give them, i.e., supplying capital, and helping in taxes, insurance, accounting, purchasing, investment portfolio, and computer applications.[41]

After the initial organization of Bankshares, the size of subsequent acquisitions became an important consideration to management. The reason was that regulatory authorities were concerned over large bank combinations, and Bankshares' management believed that acquiring a larger bank in a community would be looked on as putting the small banks at a disadvantage. They thought that if one of the small banks were acquired, however, the chances for approval would be greatly improved.

Finally, Bankshares thought that an acquisition would not work

[39] Flinn, personal communication, 1968.   [40] *Ibid.*   [41] *Ibid.*

well for either party without the full cooperation of the management of the bank being acquired.[42] They made no effort to go around management, if it happened to be reluctant to join, and talk to the big stockholders. Their acquisition strategy was to deal directly with the management of an acquisition candidate.

Bankshares' expansion strategy is clearly influenced by its small staff, which appears to be in keeping with Bankshares' philosophy of a participating management organization; a large holding company staff implies more direct control and less autonomy at the affiliate level. The choice to operate with a small staff also explains the strategy of acquiring relatively large banks that can operate without daily supervision.

The logic of Bankshares' strategy to work through the management of the bank being acquired appears well founded. Clearly, the support of the incumbents is needed if Bankshares' objective of independent operation by the affiliate is to be realized. Furthermore, acquiring a bank with a management problem is not desirable if an alternative acquisition is possible; that is, a bank where conflict is not an issue and where Bankshares may have confidence in the ability of management to operate with a minimum of supervision.

However, in a bank with profit and growth opportunities or with a key location, operating personnel may not desire the acquisition, although the stockholders wish to seek improvements through affiliation. To the extent such situations do exist, it may be desirable to deal directly with the stockholders.

[42] *Ibid.*

VI   *Legal Considerations*

THE differences in the form of corporate organization, and state regulation and other legal considerations relating to expansion, provide a major area of contrast.

Bank holding company regulation was an important factor at the national level. The Banking Act of 1933 was the first federal law affecting the regulation of bank holding companies. It has historical significance because it gave explicit recognition to such institutions for the first time in federal banking laws.[1]

Although the Banking Act of 1933 was not designed primarily to regulate group banking, it did contain provisions covering limited supervision over holding companies having control of banks belonging to the Federal Reserve System. Under this law a bank holding company is designated as a "holding company affiliate" and as such is required to secure a voting permit from the Board of Governors of the Federal Reserve System before it may vote stock of national or state member banks. Thus, the Board acquired new supervisory functions affecting both banks and the holding company affiliates controlling them.[2]

However, this regulation proved inadequate, and the Bank Holding Company Act of 1956 was passed after eighteen years of debate concerning federal jurisdiction over the operation of bank holding companies.[3]

Passage of the 1956 act opened a new era for the development of bank holding companies. It recognized this form of organization as an integral component of American commercial banking.[4] The Bank Holding Company Act of 1956 had three general objectives: " (1) to define a bank holding company in terms that cover all such companies which need to be regulated, (2) to control their expansion within limits that promote the public interest, and (3) to

---

[1] Marcus Nadler and Jules I. Bogen, *The Bank Holding Company* (New York University: Graduate School of Business Administration, 1959) , p. 11.

[2] W. Ralph Lamb, *Group Banking: A Form of Banking Concentration in the United States* (New Brunswick, N.J.: Rutgers University Press, 1962) , p. 215.

[3] *Ibid.*

[4] *Ibid.*, pp. 199–200. Forty-two separate holding companies were registered with the Board of Governors on December 31, 1960.

require divestment of non-banking interests in order to avoid certain hazards that could accompany mixed ownership."[5] The bank holding company was defined under section 2 (a) of the act as a company:

(1) That directly or indirectly owns, controls, or holds with power to vote 25 per centum or more of the voting shares of each of two or more banks or of a company that is or becomes a bank holding company by virtue of this Act, or (2) that controls in any manner the election of a majority of the directors of each of two or more banks; and for the purpose of this Act, any successor to any such company shall be deemed to be a bank holding company from the date as of which such predecessor company became a bank holding company.[6]

The other pertinent provisions of the 1956 act relate to expansion. Prior approval of the Federal Reserve Board for any holding company formation or expansion is required. Approval is based on the following factors as specified in section 3 (c) and (d) of the act:

(c) The Board shall not approve— (1) any acquisition or merger or consolidation under this section which would result in a monopoly, or which would be in furtherance of any combination or conspiracy to monopolize the business of banking in any part of the United States, or (2) any other proposed acquisition or merger or consolidation under this section whose effect in any section of the country may be substantially to lessen competition, or to tend to create a monopoly, or which in any other manner would be in restraint of trade, unless it finds that the anticompetitive effects of the proposed transaction are clearly out-weighed in the public interest by the probable effect of the transaction in meeting the convenience and needs of the community to be served.

In every case, the Board shall take into consideration the financial and managerial sources and future prospects of the company or companies and the banks concerned, and the convenience and needs of the community to be served.

(d) Notwithstanding any other provision of this section, no application shall be approved under this section which will permit any bank holding company or any subsidiary thereof to acquire, directly or indirectly, any voting shares of, interest in, or all or substantially all of the assets of any additional bank located outside of the State in which the operations of such bank holding company's banking subsidiaries were principally conducted on the effective date of this amendment or the date on which such company became a bank holding company, whichever is later, unless the acquisition of such shares or assets of a State bank by an out-of-state

[5] *Ibid.*, p. 215.

[6] *Bank Holding Company Act of 1956*, Public Law 511, 84th Congress, May 9, 1956, as amended by Public Law 89-495, July 1, 1966.

bank holding company is specifically authorized by the statute laws of the State in which such bank is located, by language to that effect and not merely by implication. For the purposes of this section, the State in which the operations of a bank holding company's subsidiaries are principally conducted is that State in which total deposits of all such banking subsidiaries are largest.[7]

The passage of the 1956 act, in addition to accomplishing the three objectives previously identified, gave bank holding companies a respectability they had lacked in the opinion of many persons both in and out of the banking business. The act removed the fear that Congress would pass a highly restrictive federal law as the result of current hearings on bank holding company legislation. In fact, this fear was identified as one cause for the great expansion of holding companies in the period just before the act.[8]

Before enactment of the Bank Merger Act of 1960, federal statutes contained relatively few guidelines regulating expansion of commercial banks by merger. The 1960 act tightened control. It provided for direct administration by banking authorities and in the public interest established broad standards to guide the administration of controls.[9] Expansion by merger was put under the supervision of the Comptroller of the Currency, the Federal Deposit Insurance Corporation, or the Federal Reserve Board depending on the legal status of the surviving bank.[10] In broad policy regarding expansion, the Bank Merger Act of 1960 followed the direction of the Bank Holding Company Act, although it incorporated slightly different legal and administrative standards.[11]

Several differences in national legislation seem to favor the merged system. While the literature gives scant attention to this area, Lewis B. Flinn, Jr. suggests that advantages to using the merged form of expansion are greater probability of approval of

[7] *Ibid.*, sec. 3 (c) and (d).

[8] Gerald C. Fischer, *American Banking Structure* (New York: Columbia University Press, 1968), p. 98.

[9] "The Banking Structure in Evolution," *Studies in Banking Competition and the Banking Structure* (Washington, D.C.: Comptroller of the Currency, 1966), p. 407.

[10] The Comptroller of the Currency has authority over merger applications if the acquiring, assuming, or resulting bank is to be a national bank or District bank; the FDIC, if it is to be a nonmember insured bank, except a District bank; the Board of Governors of the Federal Reserve System if it is to be a state member bank, except a District bank.

[11] George R. Hall and Charles F. Phillips, Jr., *Bank Mergers and the Regulatory Agencies* (Washington, D.C.: Board of Governors of the Federal Reserve System, 1964). This study analyzes current policies as related to the merger decisions by the three federal bank supervisory agencies.

merger applications, shorter time for approval, and less cumbersome procedural processing.[12]

On the basis of an examination of past Federal Reserve Board decisions, Flinn concludes that the Board rules more harshly against holding companies than mergers: "From 1961 through 1966 the Federal Reserve Board approved 79 bank holding company formation applications and denied 20, for a record of four to one. During the same period the Board approved 157 mergers and denied 15, for a record of 10 to 1."[13]

During 1963–64, according to the same study, holding company applications took considerably longer to process than merger applications. The average time was 7.4 months for the holding company and 3.2 months for merger.[14] The impact of a processing delay is illustrated by a case concerning Virginia Commonwealth Corporation. Here an acquisition offer seemingly was not acceptable to the stockholders of the bank being acquired because the market price of the holding company's shares fell during the 5.5 months of processing by the Board.[15]

Several major procedural differences in the processing of applications are said to favor the merger route.[16] The differences apply to public disclosure—also applicable to mergers where the Federal Reserve Board is the governing agency—and the possibility of hearings and resultant delays if the Comptroller of the Currency or the appropriate state agency disapproves the application within thirty days. Also, minor differences in processing applications are said to make holding companies more cumbersome to prepare.

It should be sufficient to note that the holding company applications are more cumbersome in that the Board requires information for each affiliated bank and not just for the system as a whole. In addition data on correspondent bank balances, consumer loans purchases, and municipal securities [are] called for. This information is not required by the merger forms.[17]

Another legal difference is that holding companies have a clear advantage in the acquisition of locations in Virginia.[18] As discussed

[12] Lewis B. Flinn, Jr., "Holding Company versus Branch Banking in the United States" (thesis, The Stonier Graduate School of Banking, Rutgers University, 1967) , pp. 29–68.

[13] *Ibid.*, p. 53.

[14] *Ibid.*, pp. 54–55. It was noted that recent decisions were being processed "with somewhat greater dispatch."

[15] *Ibid.*, p. 55.   [16] *Ibid.*, pp. 58–60.   [17] *Ibid.*, p. 60.

[18] *Ibid.*, p. 48; Kalman J. Cohen and Samuel Richardson Reid, "Effects of Regulations, Branching, and Mergers on Banking Structures and Performance,"

in chapter I, *de novo* branches are restricted to the immediate area of the home office, while mergers are authorized on a statewide basis. As a result, a bank merging into another community cannot branch in the area of the acquired bank.[19] By way of contrast, a holding company may acquire a bank as an affiliate, and the affiliate, remaining a separate bank, may continue to branch *de novo* in its community.

Other differences in the legal characteristics of the two forms, as discussed in the literature, concern boards of directors, the impact of reserve requirements, and contrasting methods of implementing mergers and holding company affiliation.[20] Among these the major difference involves legal as opposed to honorary boards of directors. In expansion by holding company the acquired bank retains its own board and bank officers because it remains a separate corporate entity, whereas after merger the management of the acquiring bank has to decide what to do with the board members of the acquired bank. They may appoint directors to the "big board" or to an area advisory board in an honorary capacity, or they may discharge them.

The proponents of the holding company argue that retention of the acquired bank's board keeps control of the bank at the local level in the hands of persons familiar with the problems and needs of the community. As one author states, "No bank holding company can exert a veto power over actions of the board of directors of bank subsidiaries."[21] This statement appears to be of dubious validity, however, because of the various voting control situations that may exist for holding company affiliates. Also, the legal status of affiliate directors in a holding company is thought to be the essence of decentralized management: "Though they may delegate to their officers the day-to-day routine of conducting the bank's business, they cannot delegate the consequences resulting from unsound practices and policies for which they are both criminally and civilly liable."[22] The proponents of direct merger argue that with a single board and group of officers the corporate structure is simplified and management control facilitated. The conflict in the literature ascribing virtues to centralized versus

---

Southern Economic Journal, XXIV, (October 1967), p. 236; Jerry J. Pezzella, "The Changes in the Banking Structure of the State of Virginia from 1953 through 1963" (Master's thesis, University of Pennsylvania, 1964), pp. 68–69.

[19] A merged system can merge in another community with a bank that already has its own branches and thus obtain multiple banking locations in the new area. However, further *de novo* branches would not be authorized.

[20] Finn, pp. 93–95.   [21] Nadler and Bogen, p. 22.   [22] Flinn, p. 79.

decentralized control is a matter that is not, and cannot be, clearly resolved in favor of either form. However, this issue is examined in more detail in this chapter as it applies to the banks studied.

Flinn's study, contrasting the two methods of expansion in Virginia, concludes that holding company expansion is more flexible from a procedural standpoint.[23] A holding company may expand by one of four methods: (1) acquisition of an affiliate through an exchange of stock, (2) acquisition by the phantom bank technique, (3) establishing a *de novo* branch, or (4) merger of an existing bank with one of the holding company's affiliated banks. In contrast, a merged system may expand, outside its own area, only by merger.

On the other hand, a useful feature of bank mergers in Virginia is that there is no minority interest. Under Virginia law a vote for merger by two-thirds of the stock of the merging bank—if it is a state-chartered bank—forces the exchange of the remaining stock.

While under federal statutes (12 USC 215 and 215a) dissenting stockholders of the merging bank have the right to an appraisal of the value of their shares and to receive cash payment therefor, the Virginia Statutes (Article 5 Section 13.1–68 *et seq.* of the Virginia Stock Corporation Act) contain no such provision.[24]

In contrast, acquisition by a holding company through an exchange of stock generally results in less than 100 percent ownership of the acquired bank.[25] However, to obtain total ownership the phantom bank technique may be used, under which the new bank may retain the name and charter of the merging bank, so that it would appear that the merging bank survived.

This technique uses a shell corporation, the phantom, a minimumly [sic] capitalized corporation bearing a bank name, into which the bank to be acquired is merged. With an affirmative vote by holders of two-thirds of the bank's stock the remaining one-third is forced to accept the exchange (and dissenting stockholders, where applicable, to accept cash). Then in a three-way exchange—the phantom through merger receives the bank's stock, the phantom (now a bank) issues its stock to

---

[23] *Ibid.*, pp. 60–67.   [24] *Ibid.*, p. 61.

[25] Under Internal Revenue Service regulations, 80 percent of the acquired banks' shares are needed to make the exchange on a tax-free basis. However, conditions for exchange of a minimum percentage of the shares of the bank to be acquired may be set. For example, in the exchange offer by United Virginia Bankshares (dated December 13, 1962) to its original banks 50 percent of the shares was used as a minimum. In this case the holding company wanted majority control.

the holding company, and the holding company issues its stock to the bank's shareholders—the holding company acquires 100 percent ownership.[26]

De Novo *Branching*

The critical issue regarding *de novo* branching in Virginia concerned the disparity in branching opportunities between a merged system and a holding company. The managements of both First and Merchants and Bankshares agreed that the holding company form enjoyed a significant advantage, and Bankshares preferred the holding company form for this reason.[27]

An officer of First and Merchants stated that the restriction on *de novo* branching by a merged system was probably the most valid argument in favor of the holding company.[28] However, he expressed the hope that this difference would be eliminated by legislation, which would enable a merged system to branch to the same extent as a holding company.

The impact of the restriction on *de novo* branching was illustrated by First and Merchants' operations in Lynchburg. Here they obtained six branches by merger with Peoples National Bank and Trust Company in January 1963. However, no additional *de novo* branches could be established in the area, even though the community would continue to grow. On the other hand, holding company affiliates operating in Lynchburg were able to branch *de novo* in the area whenever the need was justified. To a degree First and Merchants' expansion strategy minimized the restrictions on *de novo* branching by acquisition through merger with a bank that already had a well-established branch system.[29]

The clear advantage of the holding company over the merged system with regard to *de novo* branching applies only to the Virginia situation, since it stems from the state banking code, which is not typical of state legislation elsewhere. Moreover, the Virginia law is subject to change, although a change is not likely in the near future, if for no other reason than that the Virginia General Assembly meets only every two years.

[26] Flinn, pp. 63–64.
[27] Lewis B. Flinn, Jr., personal communication, 1968.
[28] John Green, personal communication, 1968.
[29] *Ibid.*

The consensus of the bank officers interviewed indicates that the *de novo* branching advantage of the holding company is not significant in the short run, although it could become an important factor in the long run, if the legislation is not modified. In the short run a merged system can offset restrictions on *de novo* branching by selecting merger partners with well-established branch systems. In this manner, good initial coverage may be obtained in the new market area, and since population and industrial growth patterns are generally slow to change, the structure of demand for banking services probably will not be altered in many communities for a number of years. First and Merchants' mergers in Lynchburg and Newport News added six offices in each place; fourteen were added in the Virginia Beach, Chesapeake, Norfolk areas.

In the long run, the alternatives open to a merged system to keep pace with a holding company in growing communities are additional mergers, the formation of new banks and subsequent merger, and relocation of existing branches. Each of these alternatives, however, is generally less desirable than *de novo* branching. Over a period of time opportunities for additional mergers will decline as the number of independent banks decreases and the concentration of the expanding systems increases. Often more than one merger may not be possible in a market area where there are only a few eligible banks and where the elimination of a competing bank increases concentration. For example, the Justice Department in January 1969, in challenging the proposed merger of Virginia National Bank and the Bank of Hampton Roads, alleged it would reduce competition in violation of the Clayton Antitrust Act.[30]

Also, mergers in new market areas may not be possible because of lack of banks in the area. In such an instance formation of a new bank or relocation of existing branch offices is typically a more

[30] *Wall Street Journal*, January 21, 1969. "Virginia National Bank, which the suit said is the second-largest in the state, has eight branches in Hampton Roads. It has 42% of total commercial bank deposits in the Hampton Roads area, a larger share than any other bank in the area, the suit said. Virginia National doesn't operate branches in Newport News, which adjoins Hampton Roads, but Virginia National's Hampton branches hold 12% of total commercial bank deposits in the combined Newport News-Hampton Roads area, the suit added.

"The Bank of Hampton Roads has one office in Hampton Roads and four in Newport News. It accounts for 8% of the total deposits in both Hampton Roads and in the Newport News-Hampton Roads area, according to the suit.

"Virginia National, as of June 29, 1968, had assets of $705 million, deposits of $628 million and loans of $412 million.

costly and less efficient method of entry than is merger or *de novo* branching. Thus, the long run opportunities for expansion of merged systems are not only likely to decrease, but they are also generally more costly than the opportunities for *de novo* branching of the holding company.

It may not be in the best interests of the banking public that the growth opportunities of the expanding systems are unequal in the long run. For example, merged systems may form holding companies to improve their growth potential.[31] And if merged systems are potentially more efficient than holding companies, as alleged in the literature and argued by First and Merchants, then the Virginia banking public may get higher cost, lower quality, and a reduction in banking services. On the other hand, the situation in Virginia will permit legislators and bankers to assess the relative merits of each organization if they are provided equal opportunities for growth, profit, and public service.

Reserve Ratios

A holding company, under certain conditions, could gain a lower effective reserve ratio on its total system deposits than could a merged system. Bankshares cited this point as a significant consideration.

Bankshares prefered the holding company form because of this economic advantage.[32] This advantage, representing higher potential earning power, came from two factors. First, nonmember (Federal Reserve System) affiliates operated with a 10 percent reserve ratio on demand deposits in lieu of the 12 percent (country bank) or 16½ percent (reserve city bank) ratio required for banks merged with a member of the Federal Reserve System. Bankshares' three nonmember banks gained an estimated $640,000 in earning reserves in 1964: in Bankshares' view this was potential income of approximately $38,400 per year.

Second, each holding company affiliate used the reserve ratio applicable to its own locale. Thus, only affiliates in designated reserve cities needed to apply the higher 16½ percent ratio; other banks could use the 12 percent ratio. In contrast, a merged system with an office in a reserve city was required to apply the higher ratio to

---

"The Bank of Hampton Roads, as of that date, had assets of $19 million, deposits of $17 million and loans of $12 million."

[31] In forming a holding company it may be possible for a merged system to establish previous acquisitions as independent affiliated banks.

[32] Flinn, personal communication, 1968.

total system deposits, wherever located. By not having the higher rate required on all affiliates, Bankshares in 1966 gained estimated earning reserves of $46 million. Clearly lower reserve ratios on demand deposits may be a significant economic advantage for the holding company.

The profit opportunities due to differences in reserve ratios on deposits can vary:

1. For a holding company not operating affiliates in Richmond (a reserve city) :

   10 percent ratio for nonmembers

   12 percent ratio for non-Richmond affiliates

2. For a holding company operating affiliates in Richmond:

   10 percent ratio for nonmembers

   12 percent ratio for non-Richmond affiliates

   16½ percent ratio for Richmond affiliates

3. For a merged system without an office in Richmond:

   12 percent reserve ratio for the complete system

4. For a merged system with an office in Richmond:

   16½ percent reserve ratio for the complete system

The holding company generally has a ratio advantage over the merged system. It has an opportunity, in certain cases, to apply lower reserve ratios against system deposits; that is, a member bank of a merged system cannot use the lower 10 percent ratio, and a merged system with an office in Richmond must apply the 16½ percent ratio against all system deposits, whereas a holding company with a Richmond affiliate applies the 16½ percent ratio only against the deposits of that affiliate.

This disparity in opportunities for earnings favors the holding company in acquisitions. For example, if a Charlottesville member bank were acquired as an affiliate by a Richmond holding company, the 12 percent ratio would apply to the affiliate's deposits. In contrast, if the Charlottesville member bank were acquired as a branch by a Richmond merged system, the 16½ percent ratio would apply. Under these conditions the 4½ percent differential on earning deposits would give the holding company either quicker "pay back" on its acquisition or the opportunity to pay higher premiums for the bank with the same "pay back." In either case, the difference in earnings potential gives the holding company a competitive edge in acquiring two of banking's scarce resources— desirable locations and good management.

Another effect of the differences in reserve ratios is that a major system operating in Virginia with a home office outside of Richmond, a reserve city, has an advantage in seeking entry into Richmond if the expansion is by holding company. A merger with a Richmond bank by Virginia National (home office in Norfolk) would require that the greater reserve city ratio be applied against their total system deposits. Thus, the potential earning power of these incremental deposits is lost, and the profitability of the system as a whole is adversely affected. A holding company acquisition in Richmond, however, would not affect the reserve position of other system affiliates as they are considered individual banks subject to the reserve requirement applicable to their own areas. As a result, holding company entry into Richmond is less costly and, therefore, more attractive than merger.[33]

These differences in reserve ratios generally favor holding companies over merged systems. However, changes in reserve ratios can and do take place. Consequently, the foregoing discussion is valid only as it applies to the situation reported.

It is difficult for several reasons to assess the significance of the unequal opportunities for earnings resulting from the ratios applied to demand deposits. First, the time elapsed since 1962 is not sufficient to identify the possible long-term effects on the competing forms of expansion in Virginia. Second, if there were an adverse effect on competition, it would be very difficult to assign it to the ratio differential and not to other conditions affecting competition, such as management, markets, customers, services, and organization structure.

The literature does not indicate that academicians, bankers, or regulatory authorities have expressed undue concern on this point. Because of this fact, the problem may be more theoretical than actual.

Boards of Directors

The critical question regarding boards of directors is whether, in a merged system, honorary boards of directors are as effective as the legal boards they replace. It was the position of First and Merchants that the change in status of the merged bank's board of directors was a disadvantage of expansion by direct merger. To offset the loss of the merged bank's legally constituted board of directors, First and Merchants appointed an area advisory board, using the same group of men.[34] Management found that their experience with advisory boards was especially good because the directors func-

[33] This situation would apply to other states if they had a Reserve City Bank and similar legislation regulating expansion.
[34] John Green, personal communication, 1968.

tioned as they had previously. Advisory board members were used for their advice and knowledge of the community and its affairs. The only significant difference noted by an officer of First and Merchants was that area advisory board members did not have any real legal liability.

On the other hand, Bankshares preferred the holding company form because the acquired banks retained their identity and the bank officers and directors retained full responsibility for the bank's operations.[35] The community continued to deal with the same corporate entity and corporate officers. Also, changes in existing services tended to be minimized since local management and local boards of directors continued daily supervision of the affiliate's operations. Because of these considerations, according to an officer of Bankshares, banking in the holding company approximated the required compromise between Virginia's traditional concept of unit banking and the state's need for larger banking organizations. He also argued that with affiliate directors representing one stockholder, the holding company, there was no accommodation of multigroup stockholders:

Most of our banks are 100 percent owned except for directors' qualifying shares. The exception is a very small minority whose basic rights are guaranteed by law. Naturally we safeguard them, too, for we don't want to go to court. The point is this, where you have basically one stockholder who speaks with one voice, the directors representing the stockholder, who is only one, are naturally more responsive to the stockholder's wishes. Directors do not represent different groups of stockholders with divergent ideas. Also, with only one stockholder is it not natural to be more attentive and responsive to his wishes? After all he owns the bank, lock, stock, and barrel. In a publicly owned corporation you don't have this. Neither do you have a stockholder who advises and counsels the directorate. The stockholder can't be capricious and the directors can't be arbitrary in a holding company set up.[36]

A discussion of honorary boards, also called area advisory boards and regional boards, must consider three stages in their evolution. The first is the period immediately after merger when feelings at the local level have to be considered. In this stage, the appointment of an honorary board has the negative advantage of avoiding the ill will of those members of the merged bank's old board who have not been appointed to the board of the merging bank. At this time of entry into a market area, the continuing good will of the bank's previous management would be an important factor

[35] Flinn, personal communication, 1968.   [36] *Ibid.*

in community relations, particularly if the old board members are leaders in the community.

The second stage in the development of an honorary board comes when the first new member has to be appointed, since this action inevitably raises the question of whether the board will be perpetuated. Management's decision at this point will probably depend on how effective the honorary board has been in maintaining and generating business. First and Merchants has judged its regional boards effective. In addition to appointing new members to some of its boards, a new board for Richmond has been formed.

Through their particular knowledge of local conditions and interest in the bank, members of our several Regional Boards have rendered invaluable assistance in promoting the affairs of our various widely separated offices. Recognizing this, and also that the makeup of our Board of Directors is becoming increasingly statewide in character, a new Board for Richmond offices was formed during the year. We look forward to a close association with this group of outstanding men as we do with members of the Leesburg and Virginia Beach Boards, added at the time of our recent mergers.[37]

The third step involves second generation management, if the board is to be perpetuated. The motivation of the second generation will probably be different from that of the first because of differences in their legal and honorary role in policy development and management control. The tendency will be for the development and implementation of policy to fall within the legal framework of the corporation, and for honorary directors to be kept in purely advisory roles. Consequently, it may become difficult to attract and hold the quality of person desired for such boards because top management talent is unlikely to remain content in a purely advisory capacity.[38] As a result, holding companies might have a long run advantage in competing for the best-qualified talent to fill boards at the local level. However, experience with both forms of expansion in Virginia is not of sufficient duration to evaluate this last stage in the evolution of honorary boards.

According to Bankshares, retention of legal boards is one of three

[37] First and Merchants National Bank, *1965 Annual Report* (Richmond, Va.: First and Merchants National Bank, 1965) , p. 16.

[38] Also, the legal aspects of advisory boards are not completely clear. Advisory board members may not have legal responsibility in the same direct manner as before, but they may have comparable moral responsibilities in their areas of influence. Therefore, it seems possible that advisory board members may be subject to conflict-of-interest suits in the same manner as regular directors.

reasons that holding company expansion has more nearly met the required compromise between unit banking and the need for larger banking organizations. The other reasons are that holding company affiliation does not remove a bank from the local scene, and that directors of affiliates representing one stockholder, the holding company, are more responsive than directors who have to accommodate more than one stockholder and different stockholder points of view.

Bankshares' point that changes in existing services are minimized in the holding company because local management and local boards continue to exercise daily supervision implies that local management and service inevitably change with expansion by direct merger and that the change may not be beneficial to the banking public. This is not necessarily true. New and expanded services, after either merger or affiliation, are the generally expected benefits of large system banking. Moreover, a merged system, like a holding company, may retain an acquired bank's officers, a situation that will obtain if the purpose of the merger is to acquire good management. The local banking public will then deal with the same persons even though they have different titles. And, as suggested by the proponents of direct merger, the officers in a newly acquired branch may retain the same operating responsibility or gain even more than they had before merger. In such situations the public could benefit, for example from raised lending limits at the local level.

In contrast, according to an officer of a large Virginia holding company, the customer feels that his interest is best served when he deals in the local area with the top man in a banking organization; a bank president is the top man, whereas a branch manager is not. The customer often assumes, rightly or wrongly, that the president has the authority needed to solve his problems, that referral to the home office is not required as it may be in a branch of a merged system. Retention of legal directors at the local level does not necessarily obviate outside control however. The holding company could exercise dictatorial control through the appointment of puppet boards and officers at the affiliate level. Furthermore, holding companies are open to the control of special interests in financial centers such as New York, as is any large corporation whose shares are traded on regional or national markets.

In large or medium banks the typical depositor, with a checking account or a savings account, is not likely to have a problem requiring access to the chief executive. A loan officer is likely to be the highest ranking officer many borrowers see or desire to see. In small banks, however, many customers probably like and expect direct contact with the chief executive. Even so, those customers requiring access to the president probably provide a relatively small percentage of a bank's day-to-day business, although they may be important with respect to profit. Therefore, customer access to the bank president as opposed to branch manager may not be so important as some other factors, such as the ability of any bank officer or employee to give the impression of responsive service.

The fact that holding company acquisition does not remove a bank from the local scene suggests an advantage of this form of expansion. It is evident, however, that affiliation "as the best compromise with tradition" is not a matter of principle with holding companies in Virginia. This observation is supported by the fact that in some cases, rather than acquiring a bank as an independent unit, holding companies have acquired the bank by merger. There also seems to be little difference between affiliation and merger with regard to possible adverse effects on competition; both forms eliminate a competitor and increase banking concentration. The result of either merger or holding company affiliation seems much the same to the traditional unit banker: an independent bank is replaced by a system bank.

In the matters of director response and management control, raised by Bankshares, organizational, operational, and legal considerations overlap. As concluded in chapter III, a distinction needs to be made between the situation where an affiliate is 100-percent owned by the holding company and the situation where there are varying degrees of ownership. Where ownership is almost total as with Bankshares, the action of affiliate boards can and should be more responsive to the holding company than if the ownership were substantially less. However, the question of accommodating multigroup stockholders will continue to face holding company management where any minority interest exists at the affiliate level. In fact, some bankers interviewed during the course of this research expressed the opinion that there are no more unattractive securities from the viewpoint of the stockholder than a minority interest in a small local bank controlled by a holding company. Probably the stockholder has no chance of selling his stock to anyone except the holding company, most likely on the holding company's terms. Therefore, the unattractive position of the minority interest in an affiliate appears to make holding company management vulnerable to charges from the minority. The only avenue for effective minority action may be to sue, whereas in a merged system *all* stockholders have access to a market for disposition of their shares if they disagree with management policies or actions. A dissident minority does not remain after a merger in Virginia, since an affirmative vote of two-thirds of the merging bank's stock forces the other third to exchange stock or to accept cash, whichever is applicable.

The legal differences between the situation of the directors in the two forms of expansion have definite implications regarding control and response. The functions and duties of legal directors are outlined in a publication of the National Industrial Conference Board:

> State laws under which the businesses are incorporated hold boards of directors responsible for the welfare of their companies. Directors not only are trustees of the business with a fiduciary relationship to stockholders, they also have a responsibility to the company's employees, its customers, and to the general public, upon whose good will the well-being of the enterprise depends. Failure to take cognizance of the responsibility to each of these four groups can adversely affect the solvency of the corporation.
>
> The laws do not spell out the duties of directors other than that they should manage the affairs of the company, so there are wide variations in the functions actually performed by boards of directors. However, there are seven areas of responsibility that appear to have general acceptance.
>
> 1. To establish the basic objectives and broad policies of the corporation
>
> 2. To elect the corporate officers, advise them, approve their actions, and audit their performance
>
> 3. To safeguard, and to approve changes in, the corporate assets (issuance of securities, pledge of assets on loans, declaration of dividends, and conveyance of property)
>
> 4. To approve important financial decisions and actions (such as budgets, capital appropriations, officers' compensation, and financial audits), and to see that proper annual and interim reports are given to stockholders
>
> 5. To delegate special powers to others to sign contracts, open bank accounts, sign checks, issue stock, make loans, and perform such other activities as may require board approval
>
> 6. To maintain, revise, and enforce the corporate charter and by-laws
>
> 7. To assure maintenance of a sound board through regular elections and the filling of interim vacancies.[39]

The very nature and scope of the legal director's responsibilities make the functioning of management control and director response

___

[39] National Industrial Conference Board, *Corporate Directorship Practices,* Studies in Business Policy, no. 125 (New York: National Industrial Conference Board, 1967), pp. 93–94.

in a holding company significantly different from that in a merged system. The development and implementation of policy involve resolution of problems among a number of managements, each equally and legally responsible not only to the stockholders, but also in some measure to employees, customers, and the general public. Consequently, the management process is likely to be more complex than in the merged system with its single board of directors.

Regulation

Bankshares cited three points regarding the impact of regulation on the two forms of expansion. One—flexibility in expansion—was considered an advantage of the holding company form. The other two—Securities and Exchange Commission regulations and regulatory agency control—were considered disadvantages. First and Merchants did not cite any of these points as significant.

Bankshares preferred the holding company form because it provided greater flexibility in selection of a method of acquisition.[40] A holding company could expand by acquisition of a bank as an affiliate or by merger. Bankshares' management believed that this option provided an opportunity to select the most favorable route for regulatory agency approval, an important factor in the acquisition of one of Bankshares' affiliates.

A merged system, on the other hand, had to change its charter from national to state, or vice versa, in order to change the route for regulatory agency approval; that is, a national bank could become a state member bank and thereby change the approval agency from the Comptroller of the Currency to the Federal Reserve. However, an officer of Bankshares stated that merged systems were reluctant to switch charters back and forth just to pick the agency most likely to extend approval.

The phantom bank device was an additional technique for acquisition used by Bankshares when no holding company affiliate was already operating in the area. The advantages of this method of acquisition were elimination of minority interest and exemption from Securities and Exchange Commission registration—since acquisition was by merger and not affiliation—and perpetuation of the acquired bank as the surviving bank after merger.[41]

Bankshares saw duplication of regulatory control as a disadvantage of the holding company form of expansion.[42] For example, a

[40] Flinn, personal communication, 1968.

[41] See pp. 90–91 for a more detailed explanation of the phantom bank device.

[42] Flinn, personal communication, 1968.

merged system, as a single banking institution, reported primarily to one supervisory authority for matters pertaining to examinations, branches, and incidental powers.[43] In contrast, a holding company might have a mixture of state and national, FDIC and non-FDIC, and member and nonmember banks. Consequently, in addition to being under the supervision of the Federal Reserve System, it could have all the regulatory authorities involved in supervision of its various affiliates. Under these circumstances, it was the position of Bankshares that the duplication of regulatory control resulted in minor differences in areas such as capital requirements and loan limits. Thus, policy on these matters was not uniform throughout the system.

Also, there are differences in Securities and Exchange Commission regulations. At the time Bankshares was formed (1962), banking was not subject to such provisions of the securities acts as registration and prospectus requirements, annual and periodic reporting requirements, proxy and financial reporting requirements, and insider trading requirements.[44] With the securities acts amendments of 1964, banking, for the most part, was subjected to the same securities rules as holding companies. However, banks did not have to report directly to the SEC, since they dealt exclusively with the banking agency for securities regulations, as well as other matters, while holding companies were required to report both to the SEC and to banking agencies.

The holding company may acquire a bank either by affiliation or by merger.[45] This flexibility in expansion may improve the odds of acquisition over the long run, since there may be differences in the attitudes of government agencies approving applications for expansion even though the legislative criteria for approval of merger and holding company applications are substantially the same. The holding company may then select the most likely route for approval. For example, its application may go via the Comptroller of the Currency, the Federal Reserve System, or the FDIC for merging a bank with a national, state-member, or nonmember Fed-

43 Also, each bank obviously must comply with the applicable regulations of the other authorities, aside from the areas of specific concern of the supervisory authority with primary cognizance over the bank.

44 Flinn, personal communication, 1968.

45 There are various technical differences under the Virginia Stock Corporation Act among merger, consolidation, and acquisition of assets in the sense that tax and other considerations vary. However, merger, consolidation, and acquisition of assets are considered the same under state and federal laws regulating expansion.

eral Reserve System affiliate—whichever seems appropriate. On the other hand, a merged system may apply only to its applicable agency, unless the surviving bank changes its charter in order to change the agency reviewing its application.

Flexibility in acquisitions is important to management only if the odds of approval are significantly better at one agency, and if a system is still in the early phase of its expansion program. Probably, however, management in a holding company or merged system that has reached the planned limit of its expansion would be indifferent to this consideration.

The coverage of differences in regulations in the literature is meager. It is significant that the only pertinent source found in the course of this research is a thesis by Lewis B. Flinn, Jr., secretary-treasurer of United Virginia Bankshares.[46] According to Flinn, several procedural differences make the holding company route more difficult than direct merger. Among these are the requirements for public disclosure (also applicable to merger where the Federal Reserve Board is the approving agency); hearings (with their resulting delays and uncertainties), required under the Holding Company Act if the Comptroller of the Currency or the appropriate state agency disapproves an application; and detailed information on application forms. Holding company application forms are more exhaustive, since the Federal Reserve Board requires information on each affiliated bank and not simply on the system as a whole. Information not required on applications for merger includes correspondent bank balances, consumer loans purchased, and municipal securities held. While Flinn concludes that these procedural differences make the holding company route "more difficult," it is possible that the conclusion should be, "more expensive." The marginal cost of these differences is likely to be minimal, and holding companies have specialists in their organizations to deal with the problems they involve.

Flinn cites certain technical and legal differences that work both to the disadvantage and to the advantage of the holding company. Disadvantages of expansion by holding company are that affiliation by exchange offer requires the expense of registration with the SEC and that affiliation does not eliminate minority interest, there being no minority interest in a merger. Advantages are that the holding company gains flexibility from the fact that it may purchase its own stock for use in acquisitions, and that stockholder approval is not needed to acquire new banks or issue new shares.

[46] Flinn, pp. 69–74.

The differences in regulatory agency control discussed by Flinn do not appear to be significant in the selection of a method of expansion. On the other hand, the one-bank holding company is a significant factor.[47] Managements in both types of expansion may elect to form a one-bank holding company. The essential difference under current legislation is that the regulated bank holding company will have to change the multibank aspect of its corporate structure and thereby give up the benefits envisioned in initially selecting group banking as a form of expansion. Consequently, under the current legislation, management in a regulated bank holding company cannot elect to have group banking operations and at the same time have nonbanking operations as a one-bank holding company. In making a choice management will have to weigh the benefits of diversification into nonbanking operations against the benefits of group banking. In contrast, management in a merged system may keep their banking operations in the merged form and also diversify into nonbanking operations as a one-bank holding company. This flexibility accorded to the merged system, may not be permanent, however, because of proposed legislation in Congress to extend banking regulations to one-bank holding companies.

[47] New York *Times,* September 18, 1968. The extent of the one-bank holding company movement is illustrated in a tabulation made by M. A. Schapiro and Company, Inc. In 1968 there were twenty-seven one-bank holding companies operating with $50.8 billion in deposits, or 15.8 percent of the $320.3 billion held by the Federal Reserve System's six thousand members; these twenty-seven banks also held on a capital basis $3.8 billion, or 13 percent of the $29.1 billion total. The significance of this movement is illustrated by a statement of the president of the Bank of America regarding plans to reorganize as a one-bank holding company. "A one-bank holding company presents possibilities for greater participation in a number of profitable activities, particularly overseas. While we have no specific businesses in mind, such activities might include leasing, warehousing, mutual funds, financing land development, travel bureaus and other industries closely related to finance."

VII *Conclusion: The Future*

$\mathbf{T}$HE advantage to the merged system of greater organizational efficiency is significantly different from the advantage to the holding company of greater profit and growth opportunities. Given equal opportunities under law, the potentially greater efficiency of the merged system may tip profitability in its favor.

An illustration of the artificial advantages of the holding company may be seen in the consolidation by merger of three of First Virginia Bankshares' large affiliates in the Northern Virginia area. The surviving bank was a state nonmember with a home office in Fairfax County. The new bank could establish *de novo* branches in all of the cities and counties previously open to the three affiliates, and consequently its growth opportunities were essentially the same as theirs had been. Moreover, because the surviving bank was a state nonmember, the lower (10 percent) reserve ratio applied to the combined deposits of the three banks, so that First Virginia gained approximately $587,500 in demand deposits available for loans and investments, worth approximately $35,000 in pretax earnings, if invested at 6 percent.[1] First Virginia thus reaped the potential organizational advantages of a merged system and, at the same time, the profit advantage from the lower reserve ratio, which generally favors the holding company form.

In the event profit and growth opportunities are equalized— thus eliminating the economic advantage of the holding company —the merged system may become the more viable form of banking organization in Virginia. In this lies the challenge to the banker and legislator: to create a truly competitive environment in which the holding company and merged system operate on an equal footing, and to permit the forces of competition to point to the most efficient form of banking organization, if there is only one.

---

[1] Computed on the differential between the state nonmember ratio and non-reserve city ratio of 12 percent, on the first $5 million demand deposits and $12\frac{1}{2}$ percent, on demand deposits over $5 million.

Appendixes

Appendix A

Table A-1. Twenty largest banks in Virginia, December 31, 1947

Bank	Deposits
1. First and Merchants National Bank, Richmond	$159,046,714
2. State-Planters Bank of Commerce and Trusts, Richmond	121,499,121
3. National Bank and Commerce, Norfolk	115,975,034
4. Central National Bank, Richmond	62,441,592
5. First National Exchange, Roanoke	58,292,860
6. The Bank of Virginia, Richmond	53,073,040
7. Seaboard Citizens National Bank, Norfolk	52,225,103
8. First National Bank, Newport News	29,461,578
9. Bank of Commerce and Trust, Richmond	25,970,639
10. Peoples National Bank, Charlottesville	24,635,496
11. Colonial American National Bank, Roanoke	21,158,494
12. First National Bank, Danville	19,454,966
13. American National Bank, Portsmouth	19,396,447
14. First National Bank, Lynchburg	17,926,398
15. Southern Bank and Trust Company, Richmond	17,448,422
16. Mountain Trust Bank, Roanoke	17,262,963
17. American National Bank and Trust Company, Danville	15,353,839
18. Arlington Trust Company, Inc., Arlington	15,266,900
19. Southern Bank of Norfolk, Norfolk	14,202,529
20. Lynchburg National Bank and Trust Company, Lynchburg	13,776,076
Total	$873,868,211
State total	$1,490,435,000
Percentage of state total:	
Largest five	34.7%
Largest ten	47.1
Largest twenty	58.6

SOURCE: Data from Bureau of Population and Economic Research, "Virginia Banking Survey for Years 1947, 1961 through 1966," unpublished statistics (Charlottesville, Va.: Graduate School of Business Administration, University of Virginia, 1966).

Table A-2. Twenty largest banks in Virginia, December 31, 1961

Bank	Deposits
1. First and Merchants National Bank, Richmond	$ 275,914,000
2. State-Planters Bank of Commerce and Trusts, Richmond	237,626,235
3. National Bank and Commerce, Norfolk	197,466,074
4. The Bank of Virginia, Richmond	150,974,217
5. Central National Bank, Richmond	134,856,768
6. First National Exchange, Roanoke	126,436,466
7. Peoples National Bank, Charlottesville	94,981,413
8. Seaboard Citizens National Bank, Norfolk	71,913,520
9. First and Citizens National Bank, Alexandria	62,869,455
10. Arlington Trust Company, Inc., Arlington	47,018,161
11. Old Dominion Bank, Arlington	46,785,749
12. First National Bank, Newport News	44,777,160
13. Colonial American National Bank, Roanoke	42,080,567
14. Southern Bank and Trust Company, Richmond	41,208,434
15. Lynchburg National Bank and Trust Company, Lynchburg	38,828,098
16. First National Bank, Lynchburg	34,376,097
17. Mountain Trust Bank, Roanoke	34,213,529
18. Alexandria National Bank, Alexandria	33,935,229
19. National Bank and Trust, Charlottesville	33,017,673
20. First National Bank, Danville	29,600,734
Total	$1,778,879,579
State total	$3,552,314,000
Percentage of state total	
Largest five	25.1%
Largest ten	39.4
Largest twenty	50.1

SOURCE: Data from Bureau of Population and Economic Research, "Virginia Banking Survey for Years of 1947, 1961 through 1966."

Table A-3. Twenty largest banks in Virginia, December 31, 1966

Bank	Deposits
1. Virginia National Bank, Norfolk	$ 536,086,579
2. First and Merchants National Bank, Richmond	535,156,910
3. State-Planters Bank of Commerce and Trusts, Richmond	341,038,058
4. First National Exchange, Roanoke	300,278,779
5. The Bank of Virginia, Richmond	234,201,957
6. Central National Bank, Richmond	168,170,865
7. Lynchburg National Bank and Trust Company, Lynchburg	128,176,433
8. First and Citizens National Bank, Alexandria	114,341,983
9. Seaboard Citizens National Bank, Norfolk	110,506,405
10. Old Dominion Bank, Arlington	93,672,035
11. Arlington Trust Company, Inc., Arlington	76,658,323
12. Mount Vernon National Bank and Trust Company, Annandale	65,398,057
13. Southern Bank and Trust Company, Richmond	64,821,061
14. Colonial American National Bank, Roanoke	62,843,905
15. National Bank and Trust Company, Charlottesville	62,312,984
16. Citizens and Marine Bank, Newport News	54,549,559
17. Alexandria National Bank, Alexandria	51,498,619
18. Clarendon Trust Company, Arlington	48,836,380
19. Mountain Trust Bank, Roanoke	46,836,756
20. First National Trust and Savings Bank, Lynchburg	45,946,682
Total	$3,141,322,330
State total	$5,325,334,000
Percentage of state total	
Largest five	36.0%
Largest ten	47.6
Largest twenty	59.0

Source: Data from Bureau of Population and Economic Research, "Virginia Banking Survey for Years of 1947, 1961 through 1966."

Table A-4. Growth of statewide banking systems in Virginia, 1962–66

Metropolitan areas	1962	1963	1964	1965	1966
Washington, D.C. (Virginia section)	abcd	abcd	abcd	abcd	abcde
Lynchburg	cd	cd	cd	cd	cde
Newport News-Hampton	cde	cde	cde	cdef	cdef
Norfolk-Portsmouth	bef	bef	bef	bcef	bcdef
Richmond	bcde	bcde	bcde	bcde	bcde
Roanoke	e	e	e	e	e
Other cities, with their counties					
Charlottesville-Albemarle	f	f	f	f	f
Danville-Pittsylvania			f	f	f
Harrisonburg-Rockingham				f	adf
Waynesboro, Staunton–Augusta	cf	cf	cf	cf	bcf

a: Financial General	d: United Virginia Bankshares
b: First Virginia	e: Virginia Commonwealth
c: First and Merchants	f: Virginia National

SOURCE: Data from Bureau of Population and Economic Research, "Virginia Banking Survey for Years 1947, 1961 through 1966."

NOTE: 1962 data for Bankshares are on a *pro forma* basis for the original six members.

Table A-5. Holding companies and their subsidiaries operating in Virginia as of December 31, 1961

Financial General	
Alexandria National Bank, Alexandria	$ 33,935,229
Shenandoah Valley National Bank, Winchester	13,826,507
Arlington Trust Company, Inc., Arlington	47,018,161
Clarendon Trust Company, Arlington	25,251,056
Total	$120,030,953
First Virginia	
National Bank of Manassas	$ 5,483,313
First National Bank of Purcellville, Purcellville	4,154,098
Old Dominion National Bank of Fairfax, Annandale	8,429,377
Old Dominion Bank, Arlington	46,785,749
Falls Church Bank, Falls Church	24,556,884
Total	$ 89,409,421
Total holding company deposits	$209,439,374
Total state deposits	$3,552,314,000
Ratio of holding company deposits to state deposits	5.9

SOURCE: Data from Bureau of Population and Economic Research, "Virginia Banking Survey for Years 1947, 1961 through 1966."

Table A-6. Holding companies and their subsidiaries operating in Virginia as of December 31, 1966

Financial General Corporation, Washington, D.C.	
Alexandria National Bank, Alexandria	$ 51,498,619
Arlington Trust Company, Inc., Arlington	76,658,323
Clarendon Trust Company, Arlington	48,836,380
Peoples Bank of Buena Vista, Inc., Buena Vista	2,731,933
Valley National Bank, Harrisonburg	12,523,177
Republic Bank & Trust Company, Herndon	1,280,580
The Peoples National Bank of Leesburg, Leesburg	13,761,492
The First National Bank of Lexington, Lexington	4,781,091
The Round Hill National Bank, Round Hill	5,926,481
The Shenandoah Valley National Bank of Winchester, Winchester	17,317,754
Total	$235,315,830
The First Virginia Corporation, Arlington	
Mount Vernon National Bank and Trust Company of Fairfax County, Annandale	$ 65,398,057
Old Dominion Bank, Arlington	93,672,035
Falls Church Bank, Falls Church	32,824,383
The National Bank of Manassas, Manassas	10,619,767
Peoples' Bank, Mount Jackson	4,723,345
Southern Bank of Norfolk, Norfolk	41,606,142
First National Bank of Purcellville, Purcellville	6,195,856
Bank of New River Valley, Radford	6,427,414
First Valley National Bank, Rich Creek	4,689,608
Richmond National Bank, Richmond	16,265,590
Staunton Industrial Bank, Staunton	5,825,510
Massanutten Bank of Shenandoah Valley, National Association, Strasburg	13,246,757
Total	$301,494,464
Virginia Commonwealth Bankshares, Inc., Richmond	
Washington Trust Bank, Bristol	$ 13,928,083
The Bank of Central Virginia, Lynchburg	2,409,468
Bank of Warwick, Newport News	26,214,252
The Peoples National Bank of Pulaski, Pulaski	7,764,888
The Bank of Virginia, Richmond	234,201,957
The Bank of Salem, Salem	15,668,494
The Bank of Prince William, Woodbridge	22,118,830
Total	$322,305,972

Table A-*6 continued*

United Virginia Bankshares Incorporated, Richmond

First and Citizens National Bank, Alexandria	$114,341,983
Spotswood Bank, Harrisonburg	15,934,055
Rockbridge Bank & Trust Company, Lexington	9,819,685
First National Trust and Savings Bank of Lynchburg, Lynchburg	145,946,682
Citizens and Marine Bank, Newport News	54,549,559
Merchants and Farmers Bank of Franklin, Franklin	7,603,217
State-Planters Bank of Commerce and Trusts, Richmond	341,038,058
The Vienna Trust Company, Vienna	27,363,341
Peninsula Bank and Trust Company, Williamsburg	23,673,768
Total	$ 640,270,348
Total holding company deposits	$1,499,386,614
Total state deposits	$5,325,334,500
Percentage holding company deposits of state deposits	28.1%

Sources: Data from Commonwealth of Virginia, State Corporation Commission, *1966 Annual Report of the Bureau of Banking:* Bureau of Population and Economic Research, "Virginia Banking Survey for Years of 1947, 1961 through 1966."

Table A-7. Ten largest banking organizations in Virginia, December 31, 1966

1. United Virginia Bankshares, Inc., Richmond	$ 640,270,348
2. Virginia National Bank, Norfolk	536,086,579
3. First and Merchants National Bank, Richmond	535,156,910
4. Virginia Commonwealth Bankshares, Inc., Richmond	322,305,972
5. First Virginia Corporation, Arlington	301,494,464
6. First National Exchange Bank, Roanoke	300,278,779
7. Financial General Corporation, Washington, D.C.	235,315,830*
8. Central National Bank, Richmond	168,170,865
9. Lynchburg National Bank and Trust, Lynchburg	128,176,433
10. Seaboard Citizens National Bank, Norfolk	110,506,405
Total	$3,277,762,585
State total	$5,325,334,000
Percentage of state total	
Largest five	43.8%
Largest ten	61.5

SOURCE: Data from Bureau of Population and Economic Research, "Virginia Banking Survey for Years of 1947, 1961 through 1966."

* Includes only Virginia banks.

Table A-8. United Virginia Bankshare Incorporated, acquisitions and affiliate mergers

Date	Bank	Acquired bank deposit size (millions)	Banking offices added
Original members			
Jan. 1963	State-Planters of Commerce and Trust, Richmond	$220,308	17
Jan. 1963	First and Citizens National Bank of Alexandria	61,772	8
Jan. 1963	First National Trust and Savings Bank of Lynchburg	33,520	5
Jan. 1963	Citizens Marine Jefferson Bank, Newport News	18,855	3
Jan. 1963	The Vienna Trust Company, Vienna	15,116	4
Jan. 1963	Merchants and Farmers Bank of Franklin	4,903	1
	Total (original members)	$354,474	38
Subsequent acquisitions and mergers			
Oct. 1964	Citizens National Bank of Hampton (merged into Citizens Marine Jefferson Bank and name changed to Citizens and Marine Bank)	16,635	7
May 1964	Shirlington Trust Company, Arlington (merged into First and Citizens National Bank)	12,845	3
Aug. 1965	Tri-County Bank, Mechanicsville (merged into State-Planters)	11,508	4
Dec. 1965	Peninsula Bank and Trust Company, Williamsburg	22,313	3
Oct. 1966	Rockbridge Bank and Trust Company, Lexington	9,819	2
Oct. 1966	Spotswood Bank, Harrisonburg	15,933	1
Jan. 1967	Seaboard Citizens National Bank, Norfolk (consolidated with Merchants and Farmers Bank)	110,506	15
	Total deposits	$554,031	
	Total banking offices		73

SOURCE: Data from *Annual Report* of United Virginia Bankshares (for 1963–66); secretary treasurer of United Virginia Bankshares (for 1962).

Table A-9. United Virginia Bankshares Incorporated and affiliates, consolidated

Earnings summary

Interest on loans
Interest and dividends on securities
Other income
      Total operating income
Interest on time deposits
Salaries and employee benefits
Other expenses
      Total operating expenses
Net operating earnings before taxes
Income taxes and minority interests
      Consolidated net operating earnings
Net security profits (losses) after taxes
Net loan losses before tax credit

Balance sheet summary (daily average figures)

U.S. government securities
Municipals
Loans (gross, excluding federal funds sold)
Reserve for loan losses
Deposits:
      Demand
      Time
         Total
Stockholders' equity

Average rates earned and paid (taxable equivalent basis)

U.S. government securities
Municipal securities
Total securities
Loans
Total earning assets
Total time and savings deposits

Ratios

Net operating earnings to total operating income
Net operating earnings to average stockholders' equity
Net loan losses to daily average loans
Loans to deposits, daily average basis
Year-end capital funds and valuation reserves to daily average deposits

Per share

New operating earnings
Dividends
Number of shares
Number of stockholders

SOURCES: 1967 Annual Report of United Virginia Bankshares (for 1963–66); secretary treasurer United Virginia Bankshares (for 1962).

financial summary

1966	1965	1964	1963	1962*
$ 31,750†	$ 21,304	$ 16,643	$ 13,476	$ 11,372
7,191	5,431	4,487	4,083	3,837
6,910	4,746	3,978	3,411	3,159
45,851	31,481	25,108	20,970	18,368
13,448	8,642	6,022	4,378	3,590
11,937	8,280	6,545	5,859	5,413
9,405	6,399	5,315	4,470	3,842
34,790	23,321	17,882	14,707	12,845
11,061	8,160	7,226	6,263	5,523
3,433	2,715	2,729	2,635	2,269
7,628	5,445	4,497	3,628	3,254
(1,946)	(367)	22	(143)	(849)
795	355	521	165	73
$ 85,514	$ 79,066	$ 73,484	$ 81,281	$ 89,707
94,943	67,321	49,784	39,986	33,697
497,774	349,388	274,527	233,289	201,241
8,334	5,100	3,733	2,983	2,863
$397,241	$322,435	$285,839	$271,419	$255,742
338,730	231,970	172,370	136,420	116,304
735,971	554,405	458,209	407,839	372,046
58,077	44,672	38,588	36,596	34,900
4.80%	4.35%	4.20%	3.66%	2.97%
6.28	5.73	5.77	6.02	5.60
5.57	5.00	4.81	4.41	3.67
6.30	6.10	6.06	5.70	5.65
6.10	5.66	5.61	5.20	4.87
3.97	3.73	3.49	3.21	3.09
16.6%	17.3%	17.9%	17.3%	17.7%
13.1	12.2	12.6	9.9	9.3
0.16	0.10	0.19	0.07	0.04
67.6	63.0	59.9	58.0	54.1
9.8	9.9	10.5	10.6	11.2
$3.49	$3.18	$2.91	$2.46	$2.21
1.52½	1.42½	1.25	1.20	.89
2,186,434	1,711,869	1,546,910	1,474,610	—
7,448	6,123	5,216	4,702	—

* 1962 data are on a *pro forma* basis for the original six member banks.

† Dollar amounts in 1000's.

Table A-10. First and Merchants National Bank, financial summary

---

Balance sheet summary

Demand deposits
Time deposits
Total deposits †
Loans (excluding federal funds sold)
Securities
Capital funds
Reserves

Earnings summary

Operating revenue
Operating expenses
Net operating earnings before taxes
Income taxes applicable to operations
Net operating earnings

Per share data (adjusted)

Average shares outstanding
Book value—year end
Net operating earnings before taxes
Income taxes applicable to operations
Net operating earnings
Dividends

Other significant statistics

Loans to deposits, daily average basis
Time deposits to total deposits, daily average basis
Gross earnings on loans
Gross earnings on securities, fully taxable basis
Net operating earnings before taxes to gross income
Net operating earnings after-taxes to gross income
Net operating earnings to average capital funds
Net operating earnings to average deposits
Profit (loss) on sale of securities after taxes
Number of offices at year-end

SOURCE: Data from *Annual Report* of First and Merchants National Bank for 1962–66.

* Dollar amounts in 1000's; average figures.

1966	1965	1964	1963	1962
$290,252*	$276,047	$259,485	$246,716	$197,514
210,753	177,939	146,027	127,134	80,737
501,005	453,986	405,512	373,850	278,251
315,077	272,924	235,777	209,538	141,414
132,631	125,090	122,112	121,625	98,952
43,485	39,822	37,966	35,790	26,858
8,134	7,548	6,576	5,860	4,799
$ 30,024	$ 25,037	$ 21,905	$ 19,097	$ 13,468
21,606	17,983	15,235	13,301	8,644
8,418	7,054	6,670	5,796	4,824
2,946	2,586	2,709	2,433	2,095
5,472	4,468	3,961	3,363	2,729
1,512,725	1,383,053	1,352,519	1,326,101	1,004,328
$28.82	$28.91	$28.11	$27.26	$26.14
5.56	5.10	4.93	4.37	4.80
1.94	1.87	2.00	1.83	2.08
3.62	3.23	2.93	2.54	2.72
1.60	1.42½	1.36	1.36	1.27
62.9%	60.2%	58.1%	56.0%	50.8%
42.1	39.2	36.0	34.0	29.0
6.31	5.80	5.78	5.70	5.48
5.40	4.79	4.46	4.05	3.79
28.0	28.2	30.4	30.4	35.8
18.2	17.8	18.1	17.6	20.3
12.6	11.2	10.4	9.4	10.2
1.1	1.0	1.0	0.9	1.0
($1,394,274)	$ 35,617	($334,496)	$ 32,438	$538,872
56	42	39	37	28

† Deposits acquired at the time of various mergers were in 1959, $16,296,125; in 1961, $20,204,679; in 1962, $55,058,083; in 1963, $32,758,035; in 1964, $11,022,885; in 1965, $9,726,729; in 1966, $35,300,525.

Table A-11. First and Merchants National Bank, mergers

Date	Bank	Merged bank deposit size (millions)	Banking offices added
Mergers during the period of restrictive branching legislation			
Jan. 1959	Savings and Trust Company of Richmond	$ 9.9	1
Dec. 1959	First National Bank of Ashland	6.3	2*
Dec. 1961	Petersburg Savings and American Trust Company	20.2	7
	Totals	$ 36.4	10
Mergers during the period of liberalized branching legislation			
Sept. 1962	Augusta National Bank of Staunton	$ 11.1	2
Oct. 1962	First National Bank of Newport News	44.8	6
Jan. 1963	Peoples National Bank and Trust Company of Lynchburg	32.7	6
July 1964	First National of Waynesboro	11.0	2*
Sept. 1965	Loudoun National Bank of Leesburg	9.7	3
Jan. 1966	Bank of Virginia Beach	23.9	10*
June 1966	Bank of Chesapeake	12.6	4*
	Totals	$145.8	33
	Total deposits added by merger	$182.2	
	Total banking offices added by merger		43

SOURCE: Data from *Annual Report* of First and Merchants National Bank (1962–66).

* Trust service added in this area.

Appendix B

4149 (14) When branch banks may be authorized; branches already established; how operated; penalties. —No bank or trust company heretofore or hereafter incorporated under the laws of this State shall be authorized to engage in business in more than one place, except that, (a) in its discretion the State Corporation Commission may authorize banks having paid-up and unimpaired capital and surplus of fifty thousand dollars or over to establish branches within the limits of the city, town, or village in which the parent bank is located.

(b) The State Corporation Commission may, in its discretion, also authorize banks located in any city to establish branches within other cities having a population of not less than fifty thousand inhabitants.

(c) This section shall not be construed to prohibit the merger of banks in the same or adjoining counties or of banks located within a distance of twenty-five miles of a parent bank and the operation by the merged company, of such banks, nor to prohibit the sale of any bank to, and the purchase thereof by, any other bank in the same or adjoining counties or within a distance of twenty-five miles and the operation of such banks by the purchasing bank, provided the approval of the State Corporation Commission is first had, and provided, further that at the time of such merger or purchase, each of the banks involved shall have been in actual operation for a period of two years or more, except that in any case in which the State Corporation Commission is satisfied that the public interest demands, on account of emergency conditions, that a merger or sale be effected, it may enter an order to such effect permitting such merger or sale, notwithstanding that the banks involved or one or more of them, have not been in actual operation for two or more years. The term "adjoining counties," where more than two are involved, shall be construed to mean counties each of which shall adjoin the county in which the parent bank is located.

Code of Virginia 1942, chapter 164A.

(d) This section, however, shall not apply to branch banks already established.

(e) No branch bank heretofore or hereafter established shall be operated or advertised under any other name than that of the identical name of the home bank, unless permission be first had and obtained from the State Corporation Commission, and unless such different name shall contain or have added thereto language clearly indicating that it is a branch bank and of which bank it is a branch.

Any bank or trust company violating the provisions of this section shall be liable to a fine of one thousand dollars, to be imposed and judgment entered therefor by the State Corporation Commission, and enforced by its process.

BRANCHING PROVISIONS OF THE 1948 LEGISLATION

6–26. When branch banks may be authorized; branches already established. —No bank or trust company heretofore or hereafter incorporated under the laws of this state shall be authorized to engage in business in more than one place, except that the State Corporation Commission, when satisfied that public convenience and necessity will thereby be served, may authorize banks having paid-up and unimpaired capital and surplus of fifty thousand dollars or over to establish branches within the limits of the city, town or village in which the parent bank is located.

This section shall not apply to branch banks established prior to June twenty-ninth, nineteen hundred forty-eight, nor to branches theretofore authorized by the Commission but not yet opened.

6–27. Operation of branches after merger or purchase. —The provisions of the preceding section shall not be construed to prohibit the merger of banks in the same or adjoining counties or of banks located within a distance of twenty-five miles of a parent bank and the operation by the merged company of such banks, nor to prohibit the sale of any bank to, and the purchase thereof by, any other bank in the same or adjoining counties or within a distance of twenty-five miles and the operation of such banks by the pur-

Virginia Bureau of Banking of the State Corporation Commission, *Statutes of Virginia Relating to Banks, Trust Companies, Building and Loan Associations and Kindred Businesses,* reprinted from *Code of Virginia of 1950* and the 1960 Cumulative Supplement.

chasing bank provided that the State Corporation Commission shall be of the opinion and shall first determine that public convenience and necessity will be served by such operation, and provided further that, at the time of such merger or purchase, each of the banks involved shall have been in actual operation for a period of five years or more. But in any case in which the Commission is satisfied that the public interest demands, on account of emergency conditions, that a merger or sale be effected, it may enter an order to such effect permitting such merger or sale, notwithstanding that the banks involved, or one or more of them, have not been in actual operation for five or more years. The term "adjoining counties," where more than two are involved, shall be construed to mean counties each of which shall adjoin the county in which the parent bank is located.

BRANCHING PROVISIONS OF THE 1962 LEGISLATION

6-26. When branch banks may be authorized; branches already established. —No bank or trust company heretofore or hereafter incorporated under the laws of this State shall be authorized to engage in business in more than one place, except that the State Corporation Commission, when satisfied that public convenience and necessity will thereby be served, may authorize banks having paid-up and unimpaired capital and surplus of fifty thousand dollars or over to establish branches within the limits of the city, town or county in which the parent bank is located or to establish branches elsewhere by merger with banks located in any other county, city or town.

This section shall not be construed to prohibit the operation of existing branch banks heretofore established.

The term "parent bank" shall be construed to mean the bank or banking office at which the principal functions of the bank are conducted. The location of a parent bank or of a branch bank may be moved if the State Corporation Commission determines that public convenience and necessity will be served by such move; but the location of a parent bank or of a branch bank may not be moved beyond the limits of the city, town or county in which it is located except through a merger with another bank.

Virginia Bureau of Banking of the State Corporation Commission, *The Virginia Banking Act and Related Statutes,* reprinted from *Code of Virginia of 1950* and the 1964 Cumulative Supplement.

6–27. Operation of branches after merger or purchase. —The preceding section (6–26) shall be construed to allow the merger of banks and the operation by the merged company of such banks, and to allow the sale of any bank to, and the purchase thereof through merger by, any other bank and the operation of such banks by the merged bank, provided that the State Corporation Commission shall be of the opinion and shall first determine that public convenience and necessity will be served by such operation, and provided further that, at the time of such merger the banks involved shall have been in actual operation for a period of five years or more. But in any case in which the Commission is satisfied that the public interest demands, on account of emergency conditions, that a merger be effected, it may enter an order to such effect permitting such merger notwithstanding that the banks involved, or one or more of them, have not been in actual operation for five or more years.

6–27.1. When public necessity need not be proved on application for certificate of authority under 6–31. — (a) When an application is made to the State Corporation Commission by a bank pursuant to 6–31 for a certificate of authority to commence business in a political subdivision it shall not be necessary to prove the requirements of the paragraph numbered (4) of 6–31 or, under 6–31 to prove the public necessity for banking or additional banking facilities in the community where the bank is proposed to be located when all of the banks located in such political subdivision are owned or controlled (1) by "bank holding companies" or (2) when all of the banks located in that political subdivision are owned or controlled by "merged banks" or (3) when all of the banks located in such political subdivision are owned or controlled by "bank holding companies" and "merged banks."

(b) *"Merged bank"* means any bank which has acquired another bank under the provisions of 6–26 and 6–27 which has its principal office in one political subdivision and a branch in another political subdivision.

(c) *"Bank holding company"* means any company (1) which directly or indirectly owns, controls or holds with power to vote, twenty-five per centum or more of the voting shares of each of two or more banks or of a company which is or becomes a bank holding company by virtue of this section, or (2) which controls in any manner the election of a majority of the directors of each of two or more banks, or (3) for the benefit of whose shareholders or members twenty-five per centum or more of the voting shares of each of two or more banks or a banking holding company is held by trustees; and for the purpose of this section, any successor to any such company shall be deemed to be a bank holding company from the date as of which such successor co-company becomes a bank holding company. Notwithstanding the foregoing, (A) no bank shall be a bank holding company by virtue of its ownership or control of shares in a fiduciary capacity, except where such shares are held for the benefit of the shareholders of such banks, (B) no company shall be a bank holding company by virtue of its ownership or control of its shares acquired by it in connection with its underwriting of securities and which are held only for such period of time as will permit the sale thereof upon a reasonable basis, (C) no company formed for the sole purpose of participating in a proxy solicitation shall be a bank holding company by virtue of its control of voting rights or shares acquired in the course of such solicitation, and (D) no company shall be a bank holding company if at least eighty per centum of its total assets are composed of holdings in the field of agriculture.

6–27.2 Establishment of branch banks in contiguous counties or cities. —Notwithstanding the limitations of 6–26 and 6–27, the State Corporation Commission may, when satisfied that public convenience and necessity will thereby be served, authorize the establishment of branch banks in cities contiguous to the county or city in which the parent bank is located, and the establishment of branch banks in counties contiguous to the city in which the parent bank is located. Establishment of such branches may be by merger, consolidation, purchase of assets or creation of a new branch; but if the parent bank is located in a city such branches in the contiguous county may not be established more than five miles outside the city limits.

Index

Index

American Bank and Trust Company of Richmond, 10-11
American Bankers Association, 1922 resolution of, 5

Bank holding companies in Virginia: acquisitions (1962-66), 23-24; early expansion, 16-17
Bank Holding Company Act (1956), 85-87
Banking Act (1933), 85
Banking structure in Virginia: changes in, (1962-66), 25-27; deposit concentration, 26; fewer banks, 25; larger banks, 25-26; more banking offices, 25; resistance to innovation, 27-28
Bank Merger Act (1960), 87
Bank of Hampton Roads, 92
Bank of Virginia, 3, 12-14, 20
Boards of directors, 43, 89, 95-101
Boushall, Thomas C., 4
Branches, *de novo*, 3, 8, 14-15, 19, 89-93
Branching: attitudes toward, 4, 13-14; geographic factors, 5
Buck, Fred, 18
Buck-Holland Bill, 19, 21, 29-30

Capital, flexibility in acquiring, 55, 60-64
Centralization of activities, 36, 51-52
Central National Bank of Richmond, 17
Citizens Marine Jefferson Bank of Newport News, 83
Colonial-American National Bank of Roanoke, 82
Consumer credit, 9-11; commercial banks' entry into, 9-11

Cook, A. Halsey, 11n
Credit lines, larger, 16, 71, 73

Deane, Frederick, Jr., 4n, 12n
De novo branches. *See* Branches, *de novo*
Deposit concentration, 26
Dominion Bankshares, 20n
Decentralization of activities, 41, 51-52

Economies of scale, 34-36, 48-50
Employee benefits, 36
Exchange of ideas, 37

Financial General Corporation, 16n, 20
Financial strength, 55
First and Citizens National Bank of Alexandria, 30, 83
First and Merchants National Bank of Richmond, 17; expansion strategy, 32, 77-82
First National Exchange Bank of Roanoke, 17, 20n, 82
First National of Waynesboro, 80
First National Trust and Savings Bank of Lynchburg, 83
First Virginia Bankshares Corporation, 16n, 20, 74, 105
Flinn, Lewis B., Jr., 30n, 87-88, 90, 103-4
Funds, mobility of, 53-54, 57-60

Green, John, 17n

Holland, Shirley T., 18
Holding company, advantages and disadvantages, 32